Considerations
on the Nature of the
French Revolution

Considerations on the Nature of the French Revolution

AND ON THE CAUSES WHICH

PROLONG ITS DURATION

Jacques Mallet du Pan

WITH AN INTRODUCTION BY

Paul H. Beik

HOWARD FERTIG

NEW YORK   1974

First published in English in 1793
Howard Fertig, Inc. Edition 1974
Introduction to the Howard Fertig, Inc. Edition
Copyright © 1974 by Paul H. Beik
All rights reserved.

Library of Congress Cataloging in Publication Data

Mallet du Pan, Jacques, 1749-1800.
    Considerations on the nature of the French Revolution.

    Reprint of the 1793 ed. printed for J. Owen, London.
    Includes bibliographical references.
    1. France—History—Revolution, 1789-1799—Courses
and character. I. Title.
DC150.M2513 1974   944.04   74-13491

CONTENTS

INTRODUCTION

to the Howard Fertig, Inc. Edition
Jacques Mallet du Pan: An Independent
Critic of the French Revolution

JACQUES MALLET DU PAN was an extraordinary observer of the French Revolution, a journalist who
became a participant, a foreigner who became deeply
involved. He was a Swiss Protestant pastor's son
who, as author of the political section of the weekly
Mercure de France, had spent most of the 1780's in
Paris, was appalled by the outbreak of the revolution and yet supported its early liberal possibilities.
While never ceasing to castigate the stupidities of
the counter-revolutionary Right, he himself became
a counter-revolutionist, was sent by Louis XVI on
a secret mission to the Austrian and Prussian
monarchs in 1792, and thereafter conducted, from
abroad, a confidential information service on French
affairs subsidized by various European courts. In
1797 he was driven from his Swiss refuge by
pressure from the French government and its rising
star, Napoleon Bonaparte, for supporting royalist
maneuvers within France—those which had occa-
sioned the Directory's coup of 18 Fructidor (September 4, 1797). From 1798 until his death on
May 10, 1800, Mallet lived in England, where he
published the *Mercure britannique*, largely written

by himself along lines similar to those of the *Mercure de France*.[1]

Mallet du Pan's extensive writings about the French Revolution remained for a long time half-unknown to the European public, for his secret reports to Vienna, London, and other capitals remained unpublished until the mid-nineteenth century. Thereafter, when collections of his correspondence and papers began to appear,[2] he was rediscovered and found to have something blunt and unsparing to say about nearly every phase of the revolution and counter-revolution. These writings, virtually a history of his times, were celebrated by Sainte-Beuve, Taine, Gabriel Monod, and others, and became a resource prospected by later historians, including Georges Lefebvre.

During Mallet's lifetime the reading public had been kept aware of him by the two *Mercures* and by a succession of pamphlets, each a response to some crisis. Of these writings the most famous was the *Considérations sur la nature de la Révolution de France* (1793), in which he analyzed the forces that had brought about the Republic and tried to predict their future course. Mallet's tone was relentlessly aggressive but his analytical power was formidable and his manner was redeemed by phrases that have lasted. "Like Saturn, the revolution is devouring its children."[3] Without conceiving of himself as an historian, he tried to bear witness to history and, one suspects, to fulfill an early ambition to play a part in literature. From the first he also tried to influence events, casting aside any pretense of neutrality despite his Genevan citizenship. He believed that his respect for evidence entitled him to pass judgments. In a way he was a preacher for whom truth-telling was not enough; he had to try to shape policy, vainly, as things turned out. Moreover, it was as if he had a mission to the French, a nation he viewed with extreme distaste, one would think from his writings.

Simultaneously cruel and frivolous, servile and licentious, impetuous in its complaints and forgetting them on the morrow for no reason, as light-hearted in its suffering as in prosperity, incapable of foresight or of any reflection, selling in the morning, like savages, the bed in which it must sleep that night, such was this nation throughout history, such is it showing itself to be at this moment, such will it remain until the end of time . . .[4]

Yet he was irresistibly drawn to the French and their drama, hoped against hope for its proper resolution, and devoted his best years to it, in part, to be sure, because he believed that the issues were European as well as French.

Mallet du Pan was born in 1749 in the village of Céligny, a part of the Genevan republic. Both parents—his mother's family name was Du Pan—were members of the Genevan patriciate, a commercial aristocracy with hereditary privileges. The Mallets had emigrated from Rouen to Geneva in the sixteenth century. Mallet du Pan had been a protégé of Voltaire and, like Voltaire and Rousseau, had learned about revolutions at first hand from Geneva's troubles. Through the 1780's he had worked as a journalist, first with Linguet, with whom he broke to form his own publication, then in Paris with the *Mercure* from 1784 to 1792, where he became a well known and well paid member of the literary establishment (12,000 *livres* a year by late 1789, with pension and life insurance benefits). There he won a reputation as a critic of the Enlightenment, although he denied being hostile to empirical evidence and scientific thinking. He admired Adam Smith's economic liberalism but distrusted the more abstract conceptions of the Physiocrats. Concerning government his early preferences are as elusive as those of most of his generation. He praised "experimental politics," apparently meaning incremental reforms by rulers such as Leopold of Tuscany and Joseph II. He was apprehensive about democracy well before the French revolution and was offensively disdainful of what in later times would be called the radical intelligentsia. He was cool to the American revolution and opposed French support of the Dutch democrats in their revolution against the Stadtholder in 1788. Of the French crisis of that year he wrote to a friend in Geneva that France's prospects were poor, there were too many theoretical ideas in the air and too many ambitious people around, and if the Estates General were called, there would be political demands with incalculable results.

Nevertheless, in 1789 Mallet enlisted wholeheartedly in the cause of political liberty and social conciliation led by Jean Joseph Mounier and a few other Anglophiles. Their program, identified with the two legislative chambers and the absolute royal veto destined to be defeated by the National Assembly in August and September, 1789, was an effort to balance the crown, aristocracy, and wealthy and influential commoners against each other while uniting them against the potential represented by the weight of the whole population. This strategy proved to be a mirror image of the French revolution; Mallet's fears were realized; the balance was not attained, and power cascaded from one group of political leaders to another. The Anglophiles, like other defeated tendencies, became part of that counter-revolution without which the pressures and paths of the revolution would not have been the same.

The social side of Mallet's program is suggested by the qualification he thought appropriate for deputies, something like ten thousand *livres* of annual income from landed property, and by the fact that public-spirited commoners would be allowed to sit with nobles in the upper house. For outstanding public service, commoners could win titles of nobility. There were still to be "estates," but they were to be thought of as indicators of professional functions, not "orders" with privileges. No distinctions were to be allowed that were offensive to liberty, property, or political equality, although by the latter Mallet did not mean equality of political participation, as should be clear from the ideas just mentioned; what he meant was that representation by orders, as in the Estates General, was offensive. There were remnants of corporate political privilege in Mallet's system, and they betray the terrible difficulty of implementing the Anglophile program of conciliation. He argued, further, that the traditional ranks were needed to temper the influence of "the insolent and vile aristocracy of wealth without birth, without merit,

without the emulation of honor, and without public spirit."[5] In his own eyes Mallet du Pan's revolution was not what has since been called "bourgeois."

The real revolution—the one that swept aside
his hopes—Mallet saw as a landslide of political
and social levelling and an international menace,
the product of the loss of equilibrium in 1789. By
the time he wrote his last contribution to the
Mercure, that of April 7, 1792, thirteen days before
the declaration of war, he had begun to define the
revolution as the setting free of a force that was
under no one's control. Those who had first profited
from the popular intervention were being obliged
to pay for this aid by catering to a public whose
self-confidence was growing and whose respect for
authority was declining. The early leaders were
about to be displaced, but there was no guarantee
that their successors would not suffer the same fate.
On the eve of the war he warned against war's
effects in general and the kind of reactionary war
that so many French counter-revolutionaries were
hoping for, and he was already making references
to a combined French and European solution to
the revolutionary crisis.

That spring, as Mallet was planning to leave
Paris, where his position was becoming untenable,
Louis XVI and his advisors decided to use his de-
parture for Geneva as a cover for a secret mission
to the king's brothers, who had emigrated, and to
the rulers of Austria and Prussia. It was important
to Louis XVI and Marie Antoinette that the war,
which they hoped would end the revolution, be kept
from looking like an international counter-revolutionary crusade sponsored by the French royal fam-

ily and the hotheads of the emigration. Mallet's mission was to explain Louis XVI's wishes to the king's brothers at Coblentz and to the two Central European rulers at Frankfurt. He did so, leaving Paris on May 21 and, after delays, concluding his interviews on July 18. He delivered to the Austrian and Prussian monarchs a memorandum into which he had incorporated Louis XVI's suggestions and revisions, and he urged that the powers issue a manifesto worded so that it would have the most favorable impact on internal French affairs. Sure that he had succeeded, he wrote Mounier on July 20 that Louis XVI's cause and tactics would be supported by the powers, that the émigrés would be kept on the sidelines, and that he had been able to provide a manifesto to the effect that external force would not be used to dismember France but only to help Louis XVI overcome the radicals without undoing the moderate program of reforms that the people wanted.[6]

Five days later, on July 25, 1792, the menacing Brunswick Manifesto was issued. The hard line expressed in a draft prepared by the Marquis de Limon under the sponsorship of Fersen, who was trying to represent Marie Antoinette's views, had won the approval of the Emperor and the King of Prussia. Mallet's mission had failed. It had never been as important as he believed—the intellectual briefly called to the summit—but Mallet never seems to have doubted that Louis XVI's intentions were similar to his own.

The disillusionment of the Brunswick Manifesto was shortly followed by the shock of August 10. Mallet's family had joined him in Geneva, but soon

the approach of French troops made that city un-
safe. He moved to Lausanne late in 1792, and in
the fall of 1793 settled with his family in Berne,
which was to be his observation post for the next
four years, through the Terror, the Thermidorian
reaction, and the first phase of the Directory. From
Lausanne he began to urge policies upon various
European diplomats. Most of the summer of 1793
he spent in Brussels, which was then an international counter-revolutionary gathering place. There
he wrote *Considérations sur la nature de la Révolution de France*, which was published in August,
1793.[7]

On the personal side, the book was a vindication
of Mallet's unheeded warnings, but it was also an
extravagant, aggressive counterattack on the demo-
cratic revolution and an effort to penetrate beneath
events to the forces that were producing them. In
its way it was a synthesis of Mallet du Pan's con-
clusions about the first four years of revolution, but
it was also a political act, a working paper aimed
at Europe. It went immediately through several
editions and was soon translated into English, German, and Italian. Burke said it was like something
he might have written. Mallet's acquaintance Lord
Elgin reported that it had been much discussed by
the members of the British Cabinet. Mallet was congratulated by Austrian officials in Brussels, but the
French émigrés were furious with him.

In writing the *Considérations* Mallet was probably under pressure from various people, among
them Marshal de Castries, a representative of the
French princes. As Mallet's correspondence with
him shows, de Castries was disappointed at not

having been shown the manuscript in advance of publication, and Mallet, sensitive as always about his independence, replied that his aim had been to influence the European courts, not the French émigrés; he protested that he had not brought up "any accessory question that was out of season." And: "I was requested to develop these views and make them public, in order to avoid comings and goings, endless memoirs, and private interpretations which impress too little and too slowly. I took up my pen and had the resulting piece printed. No one knew what it contained, and I had declared in advance that I would recognize no other guide than my own convictions."[8] Apparently the writing of the book had been encouraged by some of the diplomats in Brussels; his reference to being "requested" probably covers this interest as well as that of the French princes, and his statement about his independence must be presumed to apply to it as well.[9]

As an interpretation of the causes and nature of the revolution, the *Considérations* remains a faithful expression of Mallet's basic views. His analyses of social classes and political groupings are as revealing of Anglophile social philosophy as anything written during the revolution. As a critique of the counter-revolution and an effort to redirect it, the *Considérations* is indicative of the independent position that Mallet was to defend for the rest of his life; he would change tactics in the years ahead, for example with respect to the war and even foreign intervention, but would persist in his scorn for the know-nothing Right and go on preaching that the revolution was a process, was international, and had to be stopped by a coalition of realistic moderates. As for Mallet's commitment as an Anglophile liberal, one is bound to ask what was happening to it in the harsh climate of the international counter-revolution, the more so when we find him concluding with the quotation,

> For forms of government let fools contest.
> Whate'er is best administered is best.

This was perhaps a case of avoiding "any accessory question that was out of season." Whether representative government in any form should henceforth be out of season was to be a problem for all royalists in the years ahead. Although space is lacking for a discussion of Mallet's hopes and discouragements during the remainder of his career, one may report that while giving priority to the counter-revolution he was to bring to it the same will to reconcile old and new social forces that had characterized his earlier efforts on behalf of the Anglophiles. The *Considérations* is a document which stands between these earlier and later phases and expresses something of both. Mallet was to remain loyal to the monarchy without sharing the illusions of its official spokesmen, and when Bonapartism challenged his skill as a political analyst in the last year of his life, he understood it immediately and denounced its falsification of representative government, while acknowledging Napoleon's counter-revolutionary effectiveness in a cause so different from his own.[10]

Paul H. Beik

Swarthmore, Pennsylvania
June 1974

NOTES

1. The best studies of Mallet du Pan are Frances Acomb's *Mallet Du Pan (1749-1800): A Career in Political Journalism* (Durham, N.C., 1973), Nicola Matteucci's *Jacques Mallet-Du Pan* (Napoli, 1957) [in Italian], the *Mémoires et correspondance de Mallet du Pan pour servir à l'histoire de la Révolution française, recueillis et mis en ordre par A. Sayous* (2 vols., Paris, 1851), which is a biography as well as a documents collection by a Swiss historian to whom Mallet's son entrusted his father's papers, the biography *Mallet du Pan and the French Revolution*, by Bernard Mallet, the subject's great grandson, and Gaspard Vallette's *Mallet du Pan et la Révolution française* (Genève, 1893). Although, as Professor Acomb points out, Mallet himself used the spelling "Mallet Du Pan," the form "Mallet du Pan" adopted by most historians has been followed in the present essay.

2. *Mémoires et correspondance* edited by Sayous, *op. cit.*; *Correspondance inédite de Mallet du Pan avec la Cour de Vienne (1794-1798), publiée d'après les manuscrits conservés aux Archives de Vienne par André Michel, avec une préface de H. Taine* (2 vols., Paris, 1884). A third such work, appearing at the end of the century, was François Descostes's *La Révolution française vue de l'étranger 1789-1799. Mallet du Pan à Berne et Londres d'après une correspondance inédite* (Tours, 1897), which is largely composed of quotations from Mallet and his contemporaries.

3. *Considérations sur la nature de la Révolution de France et sur les causes qui en prolongent la durée* (Londres, Bruxelles, 1793), 63.

4. *Correspondance . . . avec la Cour de Vienne, op. cit.*, I, 186, report of April 29, 1795.

5. *Du Principe des factions en général, et de celles qui divisent la France.* Par M. Mallet du Pan (Paris, 1791), 26. This pamphlet was drawn from articles in the *Mercure.*

6. Sayous I, ch. XII; Appendix, 427-49 for the text of the memoir Mallet carried to the Austrian and Prussian rulers; *Mémoires de Malouet publiés par son petit-fils le baron Malouet. Deuxième édition* (Paris, 1874), Vol. II, 209-11, 219; H. A. Barton, "The Origins of the Brunswick Manifesto," *French Historical Studies*, Vol. V, No. 2, Fall, 1967, 146-168; Mallet to Mounier, from Frankfurt, July 20, 1792, in Maurice d'Irisson, comte d'Hérisson, *Autour d'une Révolution (1788-1799)* (Paris, 1888), 217-221.

7. Sayous in his generally excellent edition of Mallet's papers, Vol. I, p. 363, gives March 8, 1793, as the date of the appear-

ance of Mallet's *Considérations*, but it is evident from Mallet's whereabouts and activities, and from a passage in one of Mallet's memoirs to Lord Elgin, published by Sayous himself (II, 10) that the August date is the correct one: "Je le leur avais énergiquement prédit au mois d'août dans l'ouvrage que je publiai pour les désabuser de leurs imprudentes illusions." A typical Mallet du Pan statement! Some copies of the *Considérations*, e.g. in the Bibliothèque Nationale and the Bibliothèque Historique de la Ville de Paris, have no author on the title page, while others have "Par M. Mallet du Pan." It was certainly not Mallet's intent to remain anonymous.

8. Mallet to de Castries, Sept. 4, 1793, in Sayous I, 376-78. For background see 355-59, 375-76. Bernard Mallet, 169, says that the French princes "had not been taken into confidence" on the publication of the *Considérations*.

9. Sayous and Bernard Mallet, on the evidence of Mallet's private papers, both indicate that this was the case but do not identify the persons or the nature of their encouragement, which, if it took the form of a subsidy, makes Mallet's statement all the more important. Sayous I, 363; Bernard Mallet, 164.

10. *Mercure britannique, ou notices historiques et critiques sur les affaires du tems. Par J. Mallet du Pan* (5 vols., London, 1798-1800), Vol. IV, No. XXXII, Jan. 10, 1800, 474-75, 481; Vol. V, No. XXXIV, Feb. 10, 1800, 114-15; letters of Jan. 14 and Feb. 28, 1800, to Gallatin, to whom Mallet wrote, among other things, that Bonaparte was no General Monk: see Sayous II, 431-32, 439; letter to Sainte-Aldegonde, Feb. 27, 1800, in Sayous II, 434-36.

N O T E S

on the 1793 Translation

This original English translation of Mallet du Pan's *Considerations on the Nature of the French Revolution* is a contemporaneous document whose eccentricities suggest the era and whose occasional inaccuracies bear witness to the fact that, like the French edition, it was rushed into print in the midst of a crisis. Readers will quickly adjust to the old-fashioned letter "s" which looks like an "f" with only a faint suggestion of its crosspiece. The use of commas and some of the turns of phrase cut down on Mallet's power of expression, but his message is here. The following observations should clarify a few passages which do not do justice to Mallet's meaning. Along the way, several minor misprints and mistranslations have been noted, and the original "errata" have been incorporated into this list.

Page i of Preface, lines 19-22: "to give impressions without a determined end" might better read "to publish without any purpose."

Page ii of Preface, line 24: "In digesting" should simply be "In composing" or "In writing"

Page v of Preface, lines 17-18: after "aristocrat or democrat" (which is correct), the next pairing should be "Anglophile or Royalist" not "Monarchy or the Monarch"

Title page, in the Motto, for "remanebite" read "remanebit"

Page 3, line 11: for "these" read "those"

Page 5, line 10: delete comma between "hundred, and words"; line 11: not "conduct" but "leadership"; line 28: "these observers" should read "the observer" for the important reason that the reference is not to the foolish persons previously mentioned but to intelligent observers like Mallet himself, who appreciate the danger.

Page 17, line 29, to page 18, line 1: not "the armed chains" but "the seating," referring to that in the Legislature.

Page 21, line 25: "mobs" makes sense but isn't what Mallet wrote. He wrote "motivations" or "impulsions" (*mobiles*), which is part of a more sophisticated interpretation of the process of revolution.

Page 23, line 15: for "listen to any" read "not at all to grant it"

Page 24, third paragraph: in line 12, not "councils" but "counsels"; in line 13, Mallet is not clear whether the reference is to the conduct of the émigrés or the policies behind the foreign intervention, either or both of which would express his beliefs; in line 20, not "pretences" but "pretexts"

Page 31: in line 3 after "Government" the words "or nobility, or commoners" have been omitted; in line 5, "drawn us from" should be "has gone beyond"; and in the last two lines, "ought indeed to belong" should be "had to be the work of"

Page 37, line 24: "maxim of their tribunes" should be "tribune's maxim" without the word "their". One can't be certain, but Mallet was probably referring to the Roman tribunes, the official representatives of the plebeians.

Page 38, line 23: for "laughing" read "lolling"

Page 43, lines 22-23: not "and for the omnipotence of their delegate" but "and omnipotence for the proletarians"

Page 47, line 8: not "this diversity" but "this variant" or "this aspect" of the revolution.

Page 48, line 6: for "conficications" read "confiscations"

Page 49, lines 14-15: not "revolutionary professors" but "professed revolutionaries," which has the connotation of religious zeal.

Page 55, line 6: for "Dear" read "clear"

Page 61, line 16: for "Sovereign" read "Sovereigns"

Page 63, lines 26-28: not "undivided" but "undecided" or "indecisive"; and not "managements of neutrality" but "consideration appropriate to neutrality"

Page 64, line 25: for "ponit" read "point"

Page 66, line 5: not "constitutional" but "continual"

Page 75, line 12 of note: not "which I am to face" but "and I am prepared to face them"

Page 76, line 17: not "hoops" but "whoops"

Page 79, line 7: not "offers" but "offered"

Page 95, lines 21-22: not "of the South in Normandy and Brittany", but "of the South, of Normandy, and of Brittany". Mallet's awareness of the Midi is important.

Page 100, line 11: not "These secret proceedings" but "These misapprehensions" or "These illusions". Mallet's concern is that the French public should not believe it necessary to fight to the last against the foreign powers and the French émigrés in order to save their country from complete reaction and foreign conquest.

Page 103, line 18: for "*riguts*" read "*rights*"

Page 105, lines 13-14: an omission; Mallet's words are "right of possession made sacred by the consent of all peoples . . ." Could the "consent of all peoples" have seemed too controversial to the translator? Note also that in line 12, "men of landed property" is misleading, for Mallet says "proprietors" and means all kinds of proprietors; the idea is central to his thought. The translator makes this error in a number of places.

Page 108, lines 4-7: The important second sentence is very neatly translated, but a more literal version might help to emphasize Mallet's meaning: "The spirit of the revolution would live after it, just as it had preceded it; it has infiltrated even the minds of the oppressed."

Page 109, lines 12-20: This important passage might better read: "If any alliance, any compromise, any consideration has become impossible in dealing with that pitiless league which, for a year, has brandished its bloody knife against Paris and the Monarchy, does one not see in the common need of its interior enemies to exterminate it the principle which will soon bring together these various oppositions?"

Page 110, lines 8-9: not "combination of Kings" but "monarchical coalition"; lines 13-15: not "a detailed treaty" but "a treaty reflecting circumstances" and not just "the parties" but "the various parties". These seemingly trivial changes are important if the reader is to understand that Mallet's policy rests on cooperation between the great powers and the interest groups within France, provided the latter support a restoration.

Page 112, line 11: for "as" read "has"

Page 114, last line: for "Patua" read "Poitou"

P.H.B.

PREFACE.

VOLTAIRE, fpeaking of his own time, has faid, that one fees nothing but flimfey reafoning, mixed with a little wit. To this plague the French Revolution has fuperadded declamations without eloquence, and polemical differtations, which are copies of each other. When an Author, in a Pamphlet read by a few idlers, has ftrung together the common places which are handed about from party to party, he thinks he has amended the fyftem of the world.

This warned the Author of the Piece you are about to read, to withdraw from the combat, and quit a field where he has wafted four years in fowing on the fands. Too many Readers are in the habit of confidering writers, merely as players, who have no other tafk but that of amufing their paffions. To reafon without effect; to give impreffions without a determined end; to ftate facts to-day, which are forgotten to-morrow;---behold all that you obtain by appearing on the ftage.

　　　　　　　　By

PREFACE.

By the time we arrive at forty years of age, if we are not intirely deftitute of judgment, we place as little confidence in the dominion of experience, as in the power of reafon. The leffons of both are equally thrown away upon the people, and their rulers; and, we may efteem ourfelves fufficiently happy, if we find an hundred men in a whole generation, who derive any inftruction from the viciffitudes of human affairs.

With long intervals, indeed, there do arife Statefmen fuperior to events, which they have fkill to forefee, and the ability to prepare and to conduct *; but for the moft part, and generally, the world is governed by mere routine, or driven forward by neceffity; and Europe, in her old age, contains unfortunately, more workmen than architects.

In Revolutions, you are hard preffed between madnefs and folly; to avoid their fhock, after having paid your debt to fociety, you muft live retired, and give up, efpecially, all pretenfions to be heard.

In digefting thefe Confiderations, the Author had no higher object, than a fecret and confcientious review of his own ideas. Very
refpectable

---

* This age has produced three:—Frederick the Great; the M. of Pombal, and Franklyn.

P R E F A C E.

respectable sollicitations have determined him to publish them; which is, in other words, to abandon them to the winds. The certainty of their perfect inutility, was a powerful reason for his making no alteration in their character either by flattery or suppression, the season for both is past.

Every inhabitant of Europe is this day interested in this last conflict of civilization. Our persons and our fortunes are embarked on a vessel, every plank of which is starting, and it is not in the instant of impending shipwreck, that caution is to be left to the Master, and "working the ship, to the Crew". We are all to a man, intitled to manifest our alarms; the Revolution being, if I may so call it, *a Citizen of the World*; it is no longer the exclusive concern of Frenchmen.

The slight and transient sensibility with which the generality of mankind has viewed this tissue of guilt and infamy, which would have killed our ancestors with grief and indignation, is an additional motive, for confining our reflexions within our own bosoms. What can we say to men who sleep on beds of roses, surrounded by hundreds of thousands of assassinations; and who, with the ruins of Persepolis or of Carthage before their eyes, have never, even for a moment, conceived that empires were perishable? One must write with a red-hot iron, to excite, at this day, any sensation.

Bayle's

PREFACE.

Bayle's Problem is perfectly folved, by the prefent mafters of France. We fhall in future, know what to expect from a Republic of Atheifts; but their *timid* Revolution (this is the name they have for it) has, as yet, in other countries, but fuperficially affected the public feelings. As to the French themfelves the day is not yet come to hold up the mirror to them; their paffions fully the glafs! It is when the fad and falutary leffon of wretchednefs have made their delufion vanifh; it is then, that we fhould fpeak to fubdued and broken hearts; to underftandings difabufed by the extremity of misfortune.

The inftability of events alfo impofes filence on every man of judgment. Falfe reafoners alone have a chance of being right; for the hiftory of the time is no other than a tiffue of improbabilities. Befide, whoever has loft fight of France for fix months, has loft all knowledge of its moral and political map. The firft French exiles always fee the Revolution as at its early dawn; their remedies are fuited to times which are paft; and few there are who can form a compleat idea of the innumerable confequences, which have arifen in fo many and fuch varied epochs.

We are come to that period when the inteftine fermentation has burft open all the vents of the volcano; their crofs fires will
be

be fwallowed up and loft in the principal
gulf, if the exterior operations do not determine their direction, by enlarging their dia-
meter. The war may conduct floating opinions into one common current; but this
effect muft be feized at the very moment,
and, perhaps, it will foon be too late to
look at our watch.

I have endeavoured to develope this truth:
it will find many to contradict it, and more
who are indifferent about it. As to irritated
or irritable minds, which may be difpleafed
by this Work, the Author will put them
at their eafe by pre-informiug them, that
they may rank him in whatever clafs of
Heretics they fhall think fit; that they may
call him Ariftocrate or Democrat, a friend
of Monarchy or the Monarch, Republican
or Schifmatic; thefe titles will in no fort
hurt him: and he confoles himfelf before
hand, by recollecting, that *in the Kingdom
of Heaven there are many Manfions.*

C O N-

CONSIDERATIONS

ON THE NATURE OF THE

FRENCH REVOLUTION;

AND

On the Caufes which prolong its Duration.

THE French Revolution was neceffarily, and not accidentally the caufe of the War, and is attaining perfection by the very efforts of its Enemies. I fay *perfection*, becaufe, for fifteen months paft, dangers have to that Revolution proved refources, her fucceffes have eftablifhed her authority, and the flight checks fhe has met, have been the inftruments of her invafions. Terror has added ftrength to the immenfe force which fhe poffeffed from opinion. She has levelled every thing under the axe of her affaffins; Royalty, King, Conftitution, Laws, every faculty of Government, the law of Nature, the

B   law

law of Nations, all feeling, all remorfe, all duty; nothing remains for her to accomplifh, but the pillage of the little landed property, of which fhe ftill, and for the moment condefcends to allow the ufufruct to its poffeffors.

Thefe events are paffing in the prefence of all Europe in arms; yet the genius which prefides in her councils, five hundred thoufand valiant foldiers, eighty fhips of the line, affifted by an inteftine War, have not torn ten leagues of territory from that Confederation of crimes, which has intitled itfelf the *French-Republic!* The duration of fuch a conflict begins already to give her fome dignity. Already the public, grown callous, forgets the crimes of the Jacobins, and thinks only of their refiftance. Three months more of uncertainty, and a race of men degenerated by felfifhnefs will pafs from furprize to admiration.

If the Revolution was the caufe of the War, if its progrefs was the effect, they are now ftruggling together, body locked to body; one muft throw the other; but then, we muft obferve a marked difference between them, which is, that the Revolution may overturn the War, but the War,

in

in it's true acceptation, can never of itself
alone, overturn the Revolution.

It would then be a moft fatal miftake to
confider the exifting conteft, as an ordinary
War between nation and nation; to rely
folely upon the efficacy of the better army;
to oppofe old rules to unheard of conjunctures; to combat by meafures of mere routine
with men who have long departed from all
known modes of proceeding, and to confine
onefelf, there to perifh, within a circle of meafures, the infufficiency of which has been
made manifeft, by an experience too dangerous to be prolonged.

Vain would be the hope to draw a line
round the conflagration; it would immediately confume thefe who might be fo imprudent as to approach it. Whatever opinion
may be adopted as to the future Government
of France; of one thing we fhould never lofe
fight, that however indifferent it may appear to foreigners, whether fhe fhould at laft
fettle into a limited monarchy, or into
an abfolute monarchy, provided that either one or the other fhould reftore her to
quiet, yet Europe cannot long bear without
being infected, a *Revolutionary* Government,

with

with a treasury of all sorts of crimes, and twenty four millions of men in its train. The doctrine of the Sovereignty of the People, the investment of an indigent and frantic multitude with absolute power, liberty made to consist in respecting it in nobody; men of property subjected to starving pettifoggers, who have assumed the power of defining what property is; the tricks of a few abandoned miscreants represented as an emanation of the national will; insurrection forming the very foundation of Government, and the law considered merely as an exception in the arrangement of public order; this whole circle of anarchy, defended by arms, by perversity and delusion, excludes even an organized democracy; but it requires little foresight to perceive, from the surface they have already covered, that these dogmas and these examples will shortly and rapidly spread over all nations.

The actors in this catastrophe are at once generals of armies, political sectaries, and leaders of gangs of murderers. Their resources consist in every thing demanded by this triple character; their opinions and their decrees are made instrumental to the triumphs of their soldiers, and their soldiers to the

the eftablifhment of their opinions and their decrees; always active, always enterprizing, never diverted from their undertaking, the genius of evil feems conftantly to fpur them on. Availing themfelves by turns of promifes and of threats, of rewards and of punifhments; making always a juft eftimate of the effects of timidity, delivering to death or banifhment all who dare even to doubt, guiding all minds by half a hundred, of words they alone have fhewn any conduct, an invariable plan, and a uniform fyftem.

Unfortunately, Europe as well as France, has felt more terror than indignation at the enormities by which this domination has been both formed and fuftained. The greater number of thofe which have paffed fifty or fixty years of age, only view this Revolution through the medium of antiquated habits; they vibrate from an extravagant fear, to a falfe confidence; levity, felfifhnefs, and effeminacy, make their tranfitory alarms fubordinate to their hopes; day after day paffes away like clouds; and whilft, with their eyes fixed on the fortifications of a frontier town, they truft, with a confident fimplicity, their deftiny to an imperceptible fpot of the map, the gulph widens, and thefe obfervers

fee

fee the laft fortrefs which yet defends the remains of civil fociety, totter to its bafe.

Thefe alarms will appear no longer chimerical, when we examine their grounds; for this purpofe, I fhall bring fome thoughts before you, the refult of a chain of well-known facts, allied to the effential nature of the Revolution. I fhall afterwards analyze the principal caufes, both internal and external, which at once prolong its duration and aggravate its evils. This review of the fituation, will lead us to the confequence which it foretells, and to the meafures which it requires.

SECTION

SECTION I.

The fucceffive Progrefs, and the Birth of the Republican Revolution.

THE political reformation of the French Government has been merely the prelude, and the vehicle for that focial Revolution which threatens to be the termination of the eighteenth century. True and found philofophy had repeatedly warned and menaced Sovereigns with it: The Parifan Philofophy, unknown to the people at large, but cherifhed by the great, and by women of fafhion, conceived, combined, and carried it into effectual execution. Statefmen, and perfons of ability, had fufficiently enlightened the judgment as to the caufe of the decline of the refources of the Mornarchy, and on the manner of tempering, or of putting limits to it. But thefe modifications were incompatible with the general perverfenefs, and with the ferocious pride of a College of Metaphyfical declaimers, refolved to facrifice the prefent generation to an experiment of their maxims.

They

They drew thofe maxims from Rouffeau's *Social Contract**. The infurrection in America, fupported and juftified by an abfolute Government, put them into a perfect ferment.

* No one has formed a founder judgment on this work than Monf. *Mounier*, in his *Enquiry into the Caufes which have prevented France from being a free Country*. *Rouffeau* attributes the unlimited Sovereignty to the people, without defining at all what it is that conftitutes the people; the legiflative power to be the general will, without determining what that general will is ; he invefts this general will with the right of turning the body politic upfide down at every moment, without pointing out either forms or conditions, or limits to the expreffion of this imaginary National will. *Rouffeau* was fo imprudent, as not even to remark, that madnefs, wickednefs and injuftice could not ftamp the character of a law, on the tumultuary refolutions of the multitude. *Cicero*, a better philofopher, and founder politician, would have taught him this diftinction. If we except *Condorcet*, who hated in *Rouffeau* the refpect he entertained for the Divinity, and his averfion to the Encyclopedifts, all the Revalutionifts of France beginning with *Seyes* and ending with *Marat*, were the difciples of *Rouffeau*. The innocent blood which has been fhed for thefe four years paft fpurts back upon, and attaints his memory ; and I fear not to tell his enthufiaftic admirers, if any yet remain beyond the bloody limits of Paris, that he ought to be folemnly branded with public infamy, if the goodnefs of his intentions, and his inconfequential conclufions from his own principles, did not dictate to us fome tendernefs for his genius. The Englifh, who are far advanced beyond the reft of Europe in political knowledge, always defpifed the *Social Contract*.

ment. To read all the paradoxes which were at that time publifhed in France was quite fufficient to make us certain, if the kingdom fhould ever be agitated by difcuffions on political rights, that opinion would inftantly confound liberty with a moft perfectly unregulated democracy. To fuch a height was this delirium carried, that we have feen *Mr Turgot*, a Minifter of State, in his printed Letter to Dr. *Price*, lavifh derifion and contempt on the foundations of the Englifh Government, upon the limits by which popular power was bounded, and upon thofe inftitutions which repreffed anarchy in a legiflature.

The troubles in Holland gave vegetation to the various feeds profufely fown during the American War. In the very inftant when thefe troubles were moft highly applauded, and that it was under deliberation to arm in their favour, fome violent operations in the interior of the kingdom fet the minds of the people in a flame. Such was almoft univerfally the fpirit, that in fome of the inftructions from the affemblies of the balliages, where certain priviliges irreconcileable with even found ariftocracy were held in fanctimonious refpect, the very principles necef-

fary

fary for the confervation of monarchy in a great kingdom, were openly atttacked.

Three months had not elapfed before the National Affembly unfolded, to an obferving eye, the plan of the Revolution as it was afterwards executed. That man, who with impunity, firft ftuck the head of his fellow creature on a pike, juftified before hand the torrents of blood poured out between the 10th of *Auguft*, and 10th of *September* 1792. Crimes and errors began their career at the fame time. In a medley of men of rafh ambition, hot headed theory, and fecret treafon, a contempt for all morality foon difcovered itfelf, compounded of inftinct and calculation. Succefs appeared affured and eafy to men who reckoned as nothing humanity and juftice. Slander and violence, murder and rapine were proclaimed as lawful weapons in that warfare, which was to obtain liberty.

This project took France by furprize in a moment when effeminacy, or minds without vigour, characters debauched by luxury, manners, which were no better than bafe fafhions, opened a wide field for the Revolution. For its confummation nothing more was
neceffary

neceſſary than to unchain the ferocious
againſt the looſer vices, and to bring the effi-
minate, to battle with the brutal energetic paſſions of the multitude. Authority, which
by recent faults had been ſtripped of the reſpect of the virtuous, ſtanding alone, could
not defend itſelf from the hatred of the profligate. The firſt ſhock once given and advantage taken of it by a hardy and ſyſtematic
wickedneſs, licentiouneſs had no longer a
curb, nor its empire any limits.

This was not the end propoſed by the
greater part of the firſt Revolutioniſts. The
chiefs amongſt them ſought to diſplace, and
not to *overthrow* the public authorities. Men
of ſome parts, little underſtanding, and leſs
experience; harangues without diſcretion;
legiſlators, who killed the principle of laws,
by the deſtruction of public order, believed
themſelves to be the heads of parties, becauſe enthuſiaſtic opinion ſet its ſeal on their
diſtempered politics.

In their intoxication they did not reſerve
to themſeves any means of managing their
efforts, and of reſtraining the hands which
they had armed. To let looſe the multitude,
and to corrupt it, to erect that multitude

into

into a mighty power, and then flatter themfelves that they could make it fubordinate to
their own, fuch was the circle of follies *within*
which, in the midft of all forts of outrages on
perfons and property, the conftitution was
fabricated.

In the very inftant when the vanity of its
architects was celebrating its immortality,
even before it had feen the light, it tumbled
to pieces under its very props. An hot, but
then fecret faction, infinuated its venom,
and planted its leavers by the fide of thofe
who were fhaking the monarchy to its foundations. Its committees exifting before the
meeting of the ftates general, were fecretly
working on the plan of Milton's Satan.

" Our labour muft be to pervert that end,
" And out of good ftill to find means of evil."

The Republic, the abfolute levelling of
ranks and fortunes, the fubverfion of focial
order throughout Europe, were the fcripture
of their code. Diffembling at firft, and then
audacious, the horrors of the prefs, and clan-
deftine plots, fire and fword formed the fyftematic combination of their means of execution.

Confined

Confined at firſt to act the part of mere inſtruments, they furniſhed the founders of anarchy with the crimes of 1789. The *Palais Royal* lent its conſpirators, its corruptors and its aſſaſſins. In this alliance, the Republicans, juſt then in their birth, arranged their diſarrangements, and the council of the Duke of Orleans carried them into execution. The Revolutionary *Monarchiſts,* hoping that they alone would profit by them, ſuffered them as the ladder to a free Conſtitution.

In the boſom of ſyſtems, and of the firſt furious tranſports, aroſe that *Club of the Jacobins* which was deſtined to trample upon the heads of kings, to beat down before it all intermediate parties, and to bury all men of property, under the ruin of all Governments.

This hideous ſociety ſoon gave the law to its creators. Compelled to fear and to careſs it, in vain did they attempt to bring it to a dependance on them by the artifices of the moſt abject popularity. It eſcaped from them, and in their deſpite became the regulator of the Revolution. Whoever quitted the Club, for the purpoſe of diſputing its authority, after ſhort lived and tranſient advantages,

tages, ended by returning within its orbit, or being crufhed to pieces by it.

The *Jacobins* alone were a faction; the other parties were no better than cabals, or at moft, vegetated in impotence, whilft twelve hundred political affociations, correfponding to one common center, have from day to day ftrained clofer the knot of their union; whilft this unexampled confederation has confolidated itfelf by its cafual and temporary mifcarriages, as well as by its fuc-ceffes, its adverfaries floated on the main, without a compafs, without chiefs, without vigour, and without any common principle of harmonious agreement,

In no wife intimidated by this difcordant troop, the Jacobins marched on impetuoufly to their object. The for ever to be deplored return and captivity of their majefties in *June* 1791, gave them the opportunity of making that object manifeft.

Read their journals, their fpeeches, their petitions, their Republican Proclamations at that period; you will there find the firft edition of thofe decrees which their Committee vomited forth on the 10th and 11th *Auguft* 1792,

1792, by the mouth of *Vergniand*, in the
presence of the King, whose faithful servants
they had just murdered, and whose constitutional throne they gave to a populace of
Robbers, until they should be able to give
them his head.

The Conspiracy of *Briffot*, of *Robfpierre*,
of *Petion* and of *Condorcet*, in the summer
of 1791, gave away to the *timid* bayonets of
the General and Mayor of Paris. The Republic was adjourned to the next legiflature.
Weak men for a moment, believed the Jacobins to be annihilated. The Conftitution
revifed, but not corrected, brought on a
fufpenfion of arms for fome weeks.

With the fpirit of that prefumptuous me-
diocrity which characterifed the Conftitutionalifts, they inftantly purfued the King to
Varennes, whofe efcape would have been
their falvation, as well as that of liberty and
of the kingdom *. In the fame fpirit, and
when quitting the helm of the Revolution,
they

* Three or four of the Conftitutional leaders did not
fall into this miftake, and fincerely regretted his Ma-
jefty's arreft. Equity demands it to be told, that without their efforts, and thofe of Monf. *Montmorin*, the
Jacobins would then have accomplifhed the dethrone-
ment of the King, and the putting him on his trial.

they threw this unhappy Prince, defpoiled and naked, into the midft of Republican daggers, by ftripping him of all thofe protecting prerogatives which might have defended them and their new laws. To the unfortunate bungling of having begotten a Regicide league, without having even thought of any means to keep it within bounds, they joined another blunder, that of having created a body politic, without the means of Government.

At the opening of the fecond Affembly the Conftitution was attacked; it tumbled into pieces at every fitting; the Minutes of their proceedings were its bills of mortality; and it had vanifhed five months before it was formally deftroyed. The Jacobins performed their parts in the comedy of oaths; they alfo cried aloud, *(and laughed)*, " *The Conftitu-* " *tion or Death;*" but it was clear, from *December* 1791, that this unconnected pile could not defend its adherents, even againft the power of a Club.

This well-known fact alone paffes judgment on the Conftitution. Six months have been fufficient to fhew by experience, that being nothing elfe than an ill conftituted anarchy,

anarchy, this deformed baftard muft die in
its cradle. It muft neceffarily have expected
to have proceeded from cataftrophe to cataftrophe, under inftitutions borrowed from
fóme licentious Republics in the time of their
decline, in which infurrection was their prime
maxim; and the populace their chief fupport; in which the fovereignty of the people,
had no other controul than its own definitive will and violence; where they had fub-
mitted the public force to the force of the
mob; in which they had placed, without
any intermediate authorities, feven hundred revocable inftruments of fixty thoufand popular affembles, by the fide of a king,
altogether fuperfluous, degraded and depriv-
ed of every means to conciliate affection
to excite terror, or enforce obedience; in
which the deliberative democracy was fpread
out in the reprefentative affembly, in every
city, in every fection of a city, in the courts
of juftice, the army, in the villages, in the
clubs, in the fraternal focieties, and in every
quarter where forty banditti chofe to form a
Conventicle; in which, in a word, a majority of ten voices in the indivifible legiflature,
affured to the moft unbridled faction all thofe
triumphs of which we have been witneffes,
from the decrees for arranging the armed

D   chains

chains, to that for regulating the murder of
the King, and the funeral pomp of *Marat.*

How could the monarch and the monarchy have been preferved; Some honeft and
intelligent members of the legiflature;
their majeftics, who were daily informed of
the abominable plots which were hatching,
and a fmall number of men capable of obfervation, followed with affright the progreffive afcendancy of thofe who were determined on Anarchy. On which fide foever
you turned your eye nothing was to be
found, but inactive fears, notions without
determination, fhoals and quickfands laid
as foundations, and wordy argument difputing the field againft indefatigable action.

Thofe who wifhed to preferve the Conftitution, oppofed that phantom to a fyftem
of perfevering action; laws to a faction
above all law, metaphyfics to enterprize;
moralities to violence; fecret intrigues, to
the moft daring confpiracies; and the conftituted authorities, to a league which had
trampled all authority under foot. The
fuppreffion of the Jacobins was demanded in
a ftile borrowed from themfelves together
with their maxims, and their invectives
againft

againſt kings. Their doctrine was avowed, and its application rejected; a parade of popularity was affected in the very declamations againſt its meaſures. Thus, obſtinately implicated in a wordy war about principles and conſequences, the *Feuillans* expoſed themſelves on every quarter; beat by their own weapons, all their appeals to the letter of poſitive law were conſtantly overturned by the *Spirit of the Revolution.*

The re-embodying of men of property, ſo often propoſed, no longer afforded any hope. This inert and narrow minded maſs compoſed of ſtock-holders, of bankers, of liſtleſs annuitants; the merchants, the manufacturers, the ſmall land-holders, the jobbers in church eſtates, ſaw nothing in the Revolution but a ſpeculation of fortune and vanity. Delighted with the abolition of titles, they reaſoned juſt as the wiſeacre did, who falling from the top of a ſteeple, and finding himſelf quite at his eaſe in the air, ſaid to himſelf---*Good! provided it laſts.* Very few were maſters of ſenſe ſufficient to perceive what was of all things moſt manifeſt, which was, that after having hanged the gentlemen, they would immediately after cut the throats of the citizen; that the ariſtoc-

racy

cracy of wealth would be attacked after that
of titles and ranks, and that from the pillage
of title deeds, they would proceed to the
plunder of pocket books, and iron chests.

As to the counter-revolutionary Royalists,
they for a long time were counted for nothing. Their obstinate errors still aggra-
vated those of the *Feuillans*. From the
very beginning, the major part of the difcontented, had placed their hopes of salvation,
in the extreme of evil. They had chalked
out to themselves a commodious plan of
quiet and expectation; they took no part in
what was acting beyond some puerile attempts which, far from being able to stop
the general movement, only added to its
impetuosity. Quitting the opera, or in the
chaise which carried them to the banks of
the Rhine, men at once inattentive and
filled with passion, adjourned from month
to month the ceasing of the storm.

It was the height of absurdity to imagine
that a vast monarchy which had subsisted
for fourteen centuries, shattered to pieces in
eight days, should rise again of itself by
the progress of anarchy, by the inconstancy
of the multitude, or by some appearances
from abroad.

Alas

Alas! the root of the evil was not fo near the furface. They by whom it was planted, better underftood the human heart, and the character of the age.

Mean time they dofed over old adages and pamphlets. *" Confufion leads to order*, faid thefe profound reafoners, *anarchy will reeftablifh defpotifm. Democracy dies of itfelf, the nation is affectionately attatched to its kings."*

Thefe hackneyed fayings, true enough, perhaps, when applied to the duration of half a century, but abfolutely falfe as promifing a fhort exiftence to the anarchic fever of the French, governed the diffidents and moft of the cabinets of Europe. Never had any error more dreadful confequences, or furnifhed a ftronger proof of inexperience.

Diforder is an *effect*, which becomes an all powerful *caufe*, when it is conducted by a force not counterbalanced by any other. Neceffity compels its abettors to keep it up, and outrage begets outrage. Are laws made? They ferve to give certainty of fuccefs to every infringement of the law; at length the mobs which they raife, deftroy by their very nature all poffible means of reprefling
them

them, and for the reſtoration of order. Be-
ſides, of all forms of Government amongſt
a great people, democracy is that which
moſt ſtrongly electrifies and moſt rapidly
ſpreads the paſſions. It calls out that love
of domination which is the ſecond inſtinct in
man; give him independance to day, to-
morrow he will cheriſh it as the means of
authority, and when once eſcaped from the
power and reſtraint of the laws, his firſt
care will be to uſurp authority,

When political fanaticiſm has arrived at
this point, public order is cut off at its
ſource; for the people, delivered from an
authority which oppreſſed them, would by
the force of habit have been led toward
ſome new authority; but once ſeized themſelves with the love of power, and having
the poſſeſſion and exerciſe, it is impoſſible
that they ſhould endure any power what-
ſoever. To confirm their dominion, on
this diſpoſition, their demagogues confound
the rights of the multitude, with thoſe of
liberty, perſuade the croud that they fur-
niſh them with ideas, by inflaming their
minds, and ſubſtitute their paſſions to their
judgment, and their will to their knowledge.

How

How fuperficial then were thofe unwearied calculators who confoled themfelves by a perverted fenfe, and congratulated each other upon the encreafe of diforders, and placed all their hope in the wicked outrages which compleated the Revolution. What an enemy to royalty was that furious anonymous fcribler, who infcribed as a title on his pamphlet " *No Compromife*," and demonftrated to a majority commanding two hundred thoufand foldiers, fifty fortified towns, and in poffeffion of all the refources of the Empire, that having no compofition to expect, their deareft intereft was not to liften to any.

The Revolution is indebted to fophiftries of party fpirit, for the horrible character which it has affumed within a year paft; it owes that character to all the different caufes I have annalized; it owes it to that fyftematic emigration which feparated the monarch from his defenders; a kingdom from the friends to kingly Government, property from its owners, a party from its members, and which, unknown to itfelf, obedient to the fecret intentions of the Republicans, cut off every refource, which patience would have made fruitful in the interior of the kingdom

kingdom, without fubftituting any thing in their places.

The Revolution owes this charaƈter not alone to this meafure of emigration, which the grave and ferious nature of the anarchy fhould have confined to women, to the aged, to the heirs of the throne, to men who had evidently committed themfelves, and who were menaced by the popular rage, but fhe owes it alfo to its coincidence with the interference of foreigners.

She owes it to thofe councils which made the emigrants exclufively fubordinate to the uncertain decifions of fome irrefolute Cabinets; to that torrent of promifes, and impotent menaces, publifhed by fome fhortfighted writers, who thus fquandered away the refources to be drawn from fear; and at the fame time, furnifhed the *Jacobins* with pretences for crimes, and inftruments of dominion, when the allied army appeared on the Frontiers.

It fprung from the divifions which oftentatioufly reigned amongft the Royalifts. The Monarchy, the Monarch, every fpecies of property, three hundred thoufand families, even

even to their very hopes, were on the point
of perifhing under the ftroke of an atrocious faction; and the victims of that abominable faction were in hot difpute upon
two houfes, or three for the States, upon the
ancient Monarchy; and on the Inftitutes of
Charlemagne. An hundred idle and endlefs
controverfies daily nourifhed animofities.
Senfelefs men! they fought with one another, and they ftill fight one another with
the very chains by which they are galled.
Never could they be prevailed on to ufe the
fmalleft policy. The neceffity of hating each
other feemed to torment them; they purfued each other even into the arms of their
affaffins; neither dungeons nor death could
appeafe their animofities. Each divifion of
the party attached to monarchial Government, reprobated all thofe who did not
meet them on the geometrical line of opinion. Inftead of adjourning their debates,
inftead of ftrengthning and compacting themfelves, on thofe points in which they agreed,
they eagerly fought, on the very brink of
the precipice, to fight out the queftions
on which they were divided.

Laftly, the foreign War, fo much wifhed
for, has compleated the Revolution, which

E   it

it was intended to annihilate. Six months
fooner, a defenfive line of fixty thoufand
men would have fufficed to keep it within
fome bounds of moderation, and to facilitate
its amendment. This opportunity loft, the
armies of the two greateft military powers
in Germany, ferved merely as witneffes of
the Jacobin triumphs.

The forefight of the Jacobin leaders had
prepared this event. Affured that it would
be in vain to merely harafs the Governments of the world by infults and emiffaries
of fedition and revolt, they challenged them
to the field. Their committee, under *Briffot*'s
management, forefaw three objects of fuccefs to be obtained by a War,---the abolition
of the crown ; the deftruction of the Conftitutionalifts, to follow that of the Ariftocrates,
and all Europe in combuftion. Two of thefe
objects were obtained, and a great progrefs
was made towards the third.

Certainly fuch fharp-fighted confpirators
ftood in need only of one auxiliary, and
they found it in the contempt which was
lavifhed on them from abroad. They were
fuppofed to be filled with confternation at
the vaft military preparations, and thofe exaggerated

gerated in gazettes whilst they considered nothing in the foreign war, but as it afforded them the means of a more terrible War in the metropolis.

Answering the Duke of Brunswick's Manifesto by fifteen thousand assassinations; overturning the throne which that Prince came to defend; loading with chains that August Family, whose tears, its intended deliverers had hoped, late as it was, to dry up; they seized upon all the forces of the State---generals, authorities, administrations, ministry, revenue, laws, hangmen, newspapers, instruments of directing opinion---all became their prey in an instant : they turned against their enemies that terror, with which it was thought they themselves had been smitten, and their own confidence confirmed that of their proselytes.

If the Revolution of the 10th of *August* changed the face of the kingdom, it made at least as great a change in the campaign, begun in the moment when the very basis on which it was formed, had tumbled into ruin. Two powers only made any efforts at this crisis, in which it was to be decided whether Crwons should not be exchanged

for

for *red caps.* The deftiny of the human race depended upon a few weeks of rain or fair weather, and on the health of a few regiments. Such was the ftate to which Europe was reduced by three years of mif-taken meafures, by prefumptuous declama-tions, and by confident fecurity. Soon after fhe was hurried to the brink of ruin by the unexpected, though perhaps unavoidable re-treat of the allied army. In fix weeks the dominion of the Revolution was rapidly extended from the Alps to the Rhine, and from the territory of Genoa to the mouth of the *Scheldt.* All the hither circles of the German Empire, the United Provinces, Switzerland, Italy, all floated to the abyfs. If General *Dumourier,* whofe plans feemed to be formed in the cabinet of Tamerlane, and whom prating boafters now divert them-felves by refembling to a buffoon captain ; if this conqueror, whofe compofition was of fire and nitre, had governed the miniftry, Holland would have been in his hands in the month of *December,* and all Europe would have bowed the head before the hangmen of the 2nd of *September.*

Two hundred intriguing and peculat-ing extortioners, known at Paris by the name

name of the Committee of War; a man weak and factious who was at their head, the pillaging excurfions of *Cuftine*,---in a word, the counter-action which a prompt and vigorous genius muft ever experience in a Government of committees, were the ftar of civil fociety, by which it was faved at that time from fhipwreck *.

But by this metamorphofis the Revolution affumed another character. The fupremacy of the *Sans Culottes* confirmed itfelf on piles of carcafes, and the *Revolutionary power* became, for a murderous populace, the law of nations in regard to the people of every country. This character the French anarchy retains to this day, and it is important to confider it in this light.

* See the printed correfpondence of *Dumourier* and the minifter *Pache*. In that is to be learned the Hiftory of Europe at the clofe of 1792, and during the laft winter.

SECTION

SECTION II.

The true nature of the Revolution since 1792, and its definitive object.

" WHEN barbarians, pouring in from
" the North, overthrew the Roman
" Empire in the Weft; and when other bar-
" barians vomited out by Afia, had planted
" the ftandard of Mahomet on the walls of
" Conftantinople; that was the moment
" when the globe was to belong to the
" moft favage. In the picture of that me-
" morable fubverfion, we difcover the por-
" trait of that with which Europe is now
" threatened. The Huns and the Herules,
" the Goths and the Vandals will come
" neither from the North, nor from the
" Black Sea; they are in the very midft
" of us."

The ufurpation of France by a banditti
without bread, and by their leaders without
property, has been a comment on the
words I have cited, which I publifhed now
twenty months ago, and which were then
regarded as a mifanthropical dream.

The

The queſtion does not now turn upon a Conſtitution, or upon liberty, or upon laws, or the old or the new Government, or on a monarchy, or a Republic. The Revolution has drawn us from all thoſe kind of commotions which filled the ordinary hiſtory of nations.

Franklin often told his diſciples in Paris, that whoever ſhould introduce the principles of primitive Chriſtianity, into the political ſtate, would change the whole order of ſociety. An abſolute equality of condition; a community of goods; a Republic of the poor and of brethren; aſſociations without a Government; enthuſiaſm for dogmas, and ſubmiſſion to chiefs to be elected from their equals,---this is the ſtate to which the Preſbyterian of Philadelphia reduced the Chriſtian Religion. But to confound its divine precepts with the manners which were neceſſary to its firſt followers; but, to materialiſe, as it were, inſtitutions altogether ſpiritual, and to transform ſublime virtues into inſtruments of deſtruction and ſlaughter; this was an inference reſerved for the ſchool of the *Abbè Seyes.* The full attainment of ſuch a *ſocial renovation,* ought indeed to belong to philoſophic aſſaſſins.

Men

Men of penetrating judgment have for a long time confidered with no fmall terror, thofe legions of wretches, of journeymen, poor artifans in the fervice of luxury, for the multitude of whom Europe ftands indebted to policy derived from the counting-houfe, and to minifters drawn from philofophic academies.

The inequality of fortunes, every day growing greater, and the wafteful prodigality of an exceffive luxury, was contrafted, every day more and more, with the abject condition of a laborious poverty. By eftimates prepared by the Board of Trade and Plantations in England, upon the refults of feveral years, it appears even in that Ifland, whofe wealth and commercial intoxication have for the laft thirty years turned the heads of all the cabinets of Europe, that the condition of that immenfe clafs of people, living themfelves and fupporting their families by labour, grows worfe every day by the difproportion of wages to the price of provifions.

Almoft all the great ftates of Europe, and France more than any other, are infected by this malady.

Reflect

Reflect then on the language and the morals of the Cordelier Club, becoming the catechifm of this immenfe clafs of labouring poor; let us fuppofe a fhock fo violent as to deliver them at once from labour and dependence; behold them called to equality and power by *conftitutional* corruptors, and by them armed in an alliance with the mifcreants of every country; and fuppofe that men of ruined fortunes and blafted reputations, women loft to fhame, and all who have ambition without abilities; that the rafh and the fophifters augment and agitate this inflammable compoft; that this multitude is fattened with blood; that to them fhould be held out promifes of power and riches; that they fhould be emboldened by three years of fuccefs, and that the fanaticifm of wickednefs fhould be embellifhed by an hypocritical eloquence; when this happens, then dig the grave of civil Society, for her laft hour is at hand.

This picture is no longer hypothetical; the original is difplayed over the whole furface of France.

When you add to this that the chiefs in this enterprize, delivering the people from

F   all

all fear of divine and human juſtice, from
all ſcruple, and from every domeſtic duty,
and inſtilling into them paſſions foreign to
all their former feelings, as ſo many ſecu-
rities for their wickedneſs, have alſo been
able to corrupt corruption itſelf; what will
you then think of the idle declaimers, who
propoſe to put an end to ſuch a ſubverſion
as this, by decrees of the Great Chamber,
or by detatchments of the Gendarmerie.

This ſecond Revolution, grafted on the
firſt, has compleated the conqueſt of the
whole territory of France. The dominion
and the poſſeſſion, the ſoil and the Government, the armies and the treaſures, the
fate of all men, and the diſtribution of all
property belong, for now a year paſt to thoſe
who were excluded even by the firſt Revo-
tion from all ſhare in the public buſineſs.
Enriched by the plunder and maſters of all
public property, they have made themſelves
alſo the abſolute diſpoſers of the eſtates of
individuals, whoſe owners perfectly excluded
from all ſhare of authority, tremble in their
houſes at the ſight of ſanguinary levellers,
who conſider them merely as their farmers,

If Spartacus had been crowned with ſuc-
ceſs, he would probably have ſtopped much
ſhort

fhort of his French imitators. Amongft
thefe, Charlemagne and Mahomet would
fcarcely have obtained the rank of captains.
Their fyftem of invafion leaves far behind
it that of the Tartars, of the Arabians, and
of the Perfians into India, of the Barbarians
who difmembered the Roman Empire, who
without any violence againft private right
fhewed always more or lefs, fome refpect
for religion, for cuftoms, and for the public rights.

The Anabaptifts of Munfter, the levellers
of *Cromwell*, the wars of the peafants in
many ftates; religious Sects happily condemned at their very birth to depreffion and
obfcurity, have preceded the *Abbè Seyes* and
his demoniacs. But what a difference in the
character of the times, and in the means.
How can you compare the narrow circle in
which moved a few and inftantly repreffed
fanatics, with an empire of thirty-four thoufand fquare leagues, fubdued almoft without
refiftance, by a fweeping alliance of poverty
and crimes.

But we have as yet confidered the Revolution in one point of view only. It has an
invincible tendency to affume, it has already

F 2   affumed

affumed a fecond character, and for this it will be indebted to the War. The enthufi-aftic inhabitants and thofe without property being generally armed, ferve to maintain the conqueft it has made. France is one vaft barrack, all the Revolutionifts are fol-diers, or deftined to be foldiers; by free will or by force, the very difcontented and op-preffed themfelves, for the fake of fome chance of fafety, will be obliged to devote their arms to the defence of their tyrants. A Convention to give orders, and camps--- this is the whole of the Government in the French Republic. The reprefentatives of the people, are nothing elfe but the repre-fentatives of the army; their grand function is to rob with one hand, and with the other to fhare the plunder with the foldiers. Thus it was that *Cartouche* conducted himfelf;--- but *Attila* and *Mahomet*; the Beys of the Mammelucs, and the Scheicks of the Arabian wanderers, founded alfo their authority on a fimilar conduct.

Whilft the crowd of wife men, with whom the Revolution is nothing more than a feditious tumult, wait patiently with the countryman in Horace------*untill the river fhall have flowed out*; and whilft declaimers
amufe

amufe us by turning fentences on the fall of
induftry and of the arts, few are thofe who
perceive that the Revolution, by its deftruc-
tive nature, brings inevitably in its train, a
military Republic. Its founders could not
have taken a furer road to it, than by the
ruin of all the arts of luxury, manufactures,
foreign commerce, and every fedentary em-
ployment. Thus then, from this immenfe
body of unemployed workmen, they largely
recruit, they fupply the legions already formed of thieves and loungers, of half-ftarved
wretches and vagabonds, whom they arm
alternately with the dagger and the mufket.
By fuppreffing the workfhops, the dock-
yards, navigation, commerce and manufacture, they eftablifh for themfelves a nur-
fery of tools for their atrocities at home,
and for their regiments abroad. The foreign
war then has developed that difcipline which,
by the exclufion of all others, has reduced
twenty millions of men to two profeffions
only, War and Agriculture. Thus is verified
that maxim of their tribunes, fo often treated
with contempt, that the wealth and the power
of nations fhould hereafter confift entirely in
iron.

The time is at hand, when nothing fhall
be feen in France but the plough-fhare and
the

the bayonet. Every militant *Sans Culotte*, will be intitled to the diftribution of land and of plunder ; the fact is fo at this moment ; and prefently it will be legalized by a Conftitution in form.

One confequence will immediately flow from this eftablifhment. Thefe ferocious favages will continue armed in the midft of peace ; from the conqueft and pillage of their own country, they will proceed to their neighbours, and wafte them by their incurfions. Their policy and inftinct will unceafingly urge them to conqueft by their arms, and by their principles. It was thus that an handful of banditti collected by *Romulus*, fubjected the people of Latium, and divided the conquered lands amongft themfelves, and made their Eagle refpected from the forefts of Numidia to the banks of the Euphrates.

This picture will probably raife a fmile of pity amongft thofe innumerable idlers who over a difh of coffee, or laughing on a fopha, ftudy the Revolution in a newfpaper, and reafon on the caufes, whilft its effects inveft us in our very laft delufions. I fhall go no further than juft to beg thofe on whom
Nature

Nature has beftowed fuch beneficent compofure, to confider a little the courfe they have run. I beg of them to tell me, if from the prefent actual ftate of France, to that which I have delineated, there exifts a difference at all comparable to that between the firft and the laft epoch of the Revolution. I entreat them to bring together under the eye, the funeral pomp of *Turenne*, and that of St. *Fargéau*; the defolated Palace of the Thuilliries, with the auguft re-refidence of their Kings; the defcendant of the *Fourth Henry*, defended by fourteen centuries of monarchy; and by virtues, rarely feated by Providence on a throne, with *Louis XVI.* dragged into a dungeon by the moft infamous of the human race, murdered by the benefits which he had conferred, leaving in mourning and in chains that dear and facred family, to whom nothing now is left but the Divine protection, whilft the ftrumpets of his executioners, blaze out in their jewels in the boxes of the opera,

SECTION

SECTION III.

Divifion of the Republicans ; how they have been inftrumental to the Effects we have related.

IT would be a great miftake to believe that the revolutionary plan, fuch as it has been analyzed, was premeditated, and followed up in its totality by the rabble of factious prattlers, of thefe dictators of the kennels, and of thefe momentary chiefs, who have fucceffively given direction to a tumultuous populace. As the fpirit of the *Conftitutionalifts,* ftopped at a *democracy with a King,* fo the views of the Briffotins were bounded *by a regulated democracy of the populace.* They faw too many rifks, and too much uncertainty of preferving their own power, in the mere fimple theory of the *Sans Culottes ;* which, by reducing the art of managing civil fociety, to a fportful play of *pikes* and *guillotines,* made quite fuperfluous, the prating of *Briffot,* the anodyne admonitions of the Minifter *Roland,* the logical knaveries of *Guadet,* and that exterior of virtue with which thefe prudifh confpirators thought it expedient to adorn themfelves.

It

It will not be expected that I fhould de-
file my pen by anatomizing thofe different
fects of *decorous* butchers, or bare-faced
butchers, which were hatched in the carcafe
of the Monarchy. But, as there exifts in
Europe, and even amongft men in authority, (becaufe they are ftrangers to that moft
noble of all paffions, an abhorrence of wicked
men) a fecret and deplorable leaning to pal-
liate crimes, by the example of crimes ftill
more enormous; to feek for a fupport, in
the leaft odious party, and to eftablifh a
kind of umpirage between kindred degrees
of iniquity, we muft reduce thefe fecret
hopes to their real value; and mark thofe
fhades of difference which diftinguifh the two
factions of the *Girondifts* and the *Maratifts*.

The firft planned the Republic, and carried it into execution by the affiftance of
the fecond. It was but juftice that the Government, the committees, the directing influence, the command of the provinces, the
crown which they had feized on, that all
thefe fhould be delivered into their hands;
but they difputed with their accomplices the
municipal power which then difpofed of
lives and fortunes in the capital. The War
broke out, and it has continued ever fince.

G

The majority of the Convention were governed by the *Girondists*, juſt as the majority of the preceding legiſlature was Antirepublican. The one and the other had the ſame fate, and from the ſame cauſes. At the time of the murder of the King, the aſcendancy of the Maratiſts was fortified by the acceſſion of a kind of third party who nick-named themſelves the *independant*, and which was governed by an attorney's-clerk become a major-general, whoſe name was *La Croix*, and by one *Barrere*, a Poetaſter from Languedoc, whoſe mind was ſublimed to blood, by the manners of the time, which he dignified with the name of *Energy*.

The *Briſſotins* voted for the appeal to the people on the judgment againſt the King. Not the ſlighteſt ſentiment of juſtice or compaſſion ſuggeſted this modification; but policy dictated to them, to ſpare the Convention the odium of the King's murder, and to prevent the conſequences, which did not eſcape their foreſight. Inſtinctively and clearly they perceived, that there would be hardly an interval between the King's execution, andt heir own puniſhment.

As to their doctrines, they were promulgated in that farrago of articles and ſections
which

which *Condorcet* read one day to the Affembly, and which he embellished by a preface, every fentence of which is an abfurdity or a riddle. We perceive, that this faction purpofed to frame a Republic of Quakers without virtue, by fupplying the feeble limit of a reprefentative difcipline to an unlimited democracy; to diminifh the influence of Paris, becaufe they could no longer give it a direction; to add more force to the operation of the laws, which they flattered themfelves they fhould adminifter; to reftrain the power of the Clubs, which refufed them obedience, and to moderate that rage for blood and flaughter, with which, after having excited it, they were now threatened in their own perfons.

The *Maratifts* conceived the Revolution fuch as we have already fketched it. Leaving to their timid rivals the miferable nonfenfe of order, and of the fovereignty of the people; of refpect for the laws, and for the omnipotence of their delegate; of property maintained, and power of protecting it taken away from the propiretor;---they enforced rigoroufly *the Rights of Men.* Permanent licentioufnefs, attended with conftant impunity, under the name of Liberty; Equality

confecrated

confecrated by Agrarian laws, extended to goods and pocket books; the guillotine and the dagger for thofe who refift;---this is their code; and they enact a chapter of it every day.

It would be a great miftake to fuppofe that the *Briffotins* were more fcrupulous *. More dexterous, lefs ferocious; not fo head-long as their adverfaries, they excell them in Machiavelian policy. They have the art to adapt their bufinefs in all its circumftances to the crime to be perpetrated, and leave to their rivals the bad policy of committing more crimes than are called for by the cir-cumftances of their affairs; the *Briffotin* meafure for wickednefs is afcertained with the utmoft precifion.

If the *Briffotins* are better politicians, the *Maratifts* have a more daring fpirit. Thefe boldly plunge into blood without difguife, whilft the *Briffotins* fhed it drop by drop, with their hands covered, a mafk on their face,

* There do, no doubt, exift fome Republicans of a better defcription, who are intimidated by civic butcheries, or difabufed by them ; but you cannot bring into active fervice, a defcription of men, condemned by their nature, to be the fport of all parties.

face, and morality in their mouths. Their moderation is the effect of fear, and not of conscience; and if they have not dared the extremes of wickedness, it is because they saw that in pushing these extremes against the others, they set an example, and justified the most violent and desperate of factions in the use of the same extremities against themselves *.

The

* The Brissotines play a double game; by one, they provoke to all manner of crimes, when crimes are for their advantage; by the other, they reprobate these very crimes when their own party is endangered by them. When *Jourdan* opened the-ice. houses of Avignon, to fill them with the murdered bodies of his victims, *Brissot* immediately published in his Journal, " That the murderers had not much to reproach them- " selves with; that crimes inseparable from a Revolu- " tion have a tendency to the public welfare; and be- " sides, that it was *almost* the intire nation, or at least " a *very great part of it*, that inflicted punishment by " violence, upon some individuals, who by a *criminal* " *resistance*, opposed the *general will*, suddenly, and " *tumultuously* expressed." In consequence of this, *La-source, Guadet, Graugeneuve*, accomplices and associates of the *virtuous Brissot*, obtained an act of indemnity for the murders at Avignon. Again, it was this same *Brissot*, the *respectable friend* of Lord Lauderdale, who, when his rival Journalists were plundered, and guillotined, cried out, that *we must accommodate ourselves to the circum-stances of the time, and let the law sleep for a while*; but when, this last spring, the *Commune* of Paris proscribed the Journal published by this *Brissot*, then instantly

The differences between thefe two parties were fuch as to infure victory to that which was moft favage. Rendered unpopular, by the very efforts they made to appear popular,

Virtue, Morality, Order, Equality, Liberty, all were fhaken to the foundation. Further, this was the very Briffot, who made it his folemn boaft, that he brought on the War, for the purpofe, on the firft mifcarriage, of accufing the King of collufion with the enemy, and hurling him from the throne.

Every one is acquainted with the maxims of the virtuous Petion, whofe life-guard, difpatched from Paris, murdered the Duke of Rochefoucault, juft in the fame manner as the auftere virtue of Briffot had delivered the throats of Mr. Montmorin, and Mr. Leffart to the knives of the murderers of the 2nd and 3d of September.

The third of this triumvirate of the 10th of Auguft, the virtuous Roland, fpeaking of the maffacres in September, thus expreffed himfelf to the Parifians; " I " well forefaw what the long and abufed patience of the " people, as well as their Juftice muft naturally pro-" duce. I was not difpofed inconfiderately to blame " the firft violence of a terrible commotion; but " thought that its continuance was to be avoided. Juft " as a great tempeft purifies the air, and fweeps away " all filth, fo does popular rage and commotion, effect " that in a few hours, which in the regular courfe of " affairs, would come perhaps too late."

Thefe then are the men who at this day follicit compaffion, becaufe their crimes fall back upon their own heads, and who pretended to weep over, after they had immolated their victims, becaufe Danton and Roberfpierre, iffued out, againft them alfo, Warrants of Arreft.

Every

pular, the Briſſotins, in this battle of vultures, left every day a feather on the field of battle. Having loſt piece by piece their paltry outworks, they ſaw the citadel of their *inviolability* carried by ſtorm, by the very ſame arms with which they had attacked the inviolability of the King.

This diverſity in the Revolution, was the reſult, as were the preceding, not of a great and ſudden *coup de main,* but of a thouſand detailed preparations. The *Jacobins* gnawed the barricado, which they were afraid of attacking by main force. During the ſeveral debates, and in the midſt of the Jeremiah-like lamentations of *Roland* the dethroned ; ſolemn

Every one knows that the Aſſembly *unanimouſly* paſſed to the order of the day, when they were called upon to attend to the maſſacre in the priſons. Not one of the conſtituted authorities took a ſtep in the buſineſs; but *Roland,* the miniſter for the home department, wrote to *Santerre* on the 4th of *September,* that is, two days after the compleat perpetration of crimes never heard of in the annals of human wickedneſs, " *To employ the whole* " *force which the law had put into his hands, for the protection* " *of perſons and property.*"

The length of this note will be juſtified by the neceſſity of undeceiving thoſe, who were ſo indulgent as to ſuppoſe that the authors of the proceedings on the 10th of *Auguſt,* had an iota more of integrity, than their rivals of the 2nd of *September.*

solemn maffacres, such as those of the 2nd of *September*, were legitimatized; the invasion of property was decreed at the Club of the *Jacobins*, by the *Commune* of Paris, and by the *Mountain*; the forced loans, and the conficications were carried into execution; the Revolutionary Tribunal took firm root in its own maffacres; Paris, and the whole kingdom. was one vaft *Slaughter-houfe* *; indifcreet language became a capital crime, and conduct, in itfelf quite indifferent, rebellion; every citizen, who was not a Jacobin, was devoted to pillage, to a dungeon, or to death. Special Commiffioners were fent into all the departments for the purpofe of extermination †. Journeymen hangmen

---

In the original the word is *Geoménie*, alluding to thofe ftairs leading down to the *Tiber*, called *Scalæ Gemoniæ*, on which tyrannical princes, and profcribing factions, expofed to public ignominy, the bodies of thofe whom they had murdered. Thefe bodies were, after a time, thrown into the river. The word is unufual and harfh in the French, and cannot be at all rendered into Englifh. Another, fufficiently expreffive of the Author's fenfe is fubftituted.

† The department and the judges of *Ain*, having reprefented to them that they could not, without fome evidence, put to death a crowd of Citizens of all conditions imprifoned at *Bourg*; thefe Commiffioners, gnafhing their teeth, anfwered—"*Eh! if we had required* "*evidence, fhould weh ave condemned* CAPET?"

hangmen filled the adminiftration, and had
no other part to play but that of *Mutes* in
the Affembly. In a word, that Affembly
affumed the charaéter of roaring tygers broke
loofe. Never did the *Bicetre* exhibit more
of abomination and horrors; the moft profligate mifcreants in a night-cellar might
have paffed for the Roman Senate in com-
parifon with that den at the Thuilliries,
where the refufe of the gallows diétated decrees to the dregs of human nature, and
where buffoon cannibals challenged each
other to glaffes of blood *.

Now then the theory of revolutionary
profeffors is in full praétice, and has but two
more obftacles to furmount, the revolts
within the kingdom, and the War from
without; thefe will confirm the Republic of
Sans Cullottes, if they fhould not be able to
give it its death blow before winter.

* " *Bring a glafs of blood to* Couthon," faid lately,
one of the members on the right fide of the hall,
" *Bring a tub of patriotic blood, for a bath, for thefe gen-*
" *tlemen*," replied the left fide.

H   SECTION

SECTION IV.

Views of the Republicans in the present War;
how it regards the Revolution; Causes of
Resistance.

THE Revolution and the War are infe-
parable; they have the same origin; all
the means of Revolutions are means of war;
and it is beyond human power to diffolve
this alliance, if the principle is fuffered to
efcape.

In provoking and fpreading fo generally
this terrible conflict, the Republicans had
fix objects, all in correfpondence, one with
the other.

To confirm the French Revolution, and
to make it a Revolution in all civilized
focieties.

Not to leave a throne ftanding, nor any
government whatfoever, which refted on
any other foundation, than that of an unlimited military, aud deliberative democracy.

To level all diftinctions, and to rob all
men of landed eftates, the gentry, after the
clergy,

clergy, the yeomanry after the gentry, the monied men after the yeomanry, the merchants as well as the monied men, and the stock-holder after the merchant.

To crush the land-owners by excessive and arbitrary contributions, until the moment arrived for violently expelling them from their patrimonies.

To accomplish this, by giving to the *Sans Cullottes* exclusively, the sovereignty, the power, the armies, the offices, and the treasuries of the kingdom.

Lastly, to incorporate with them all conquered countries, by realising in those countries, the French measures; to feed the War by plunder, and to support plunder by the War.

The famous decrees of the 15th and 30th of *December* last, decrees which containing the recapitulation, the system, and the result of the Revolution, bear directly on these six elementary objects. From them *Cambon* composed his preliminary discourse, in which all disguise was thrown aside. Transported with admiration, the Assembly eagerly and without

delay

delay difpatched traders in liberty, under the name of Commiffioners to go, and *fraternally* to fell the *Rights of Man* at the foot of the Alps, on the banks of the Rhine, the Meufe and the Scheldt, to ftock-job in confifcations ; and after making the people pay the full price of the independence which they brought to them, then fword in hand, to adjudge their countries to France, by *voluntary* re-unions.

Although, the change of fortune in the fpring has a little difordered the oeconomy of this philofophical generofity, yet would it be a great miftake to fuppofe the plan to be abandoned. Foreign armies do indeed *cramp* its operation for the prefent, but its fpirit is in full force. Never has the *propofition* of evacuating what is yet in their hands of the conquered country, been well received in the Convention, and there can be no doubt, that on their very firft fuccefs or after a treacherous peace of four and twenty hours, the *Cambons* will again make their appearance, with the *Gengis-kans* of the fraternal focieties.

If the two factions fhould come to a recon-ciliation, the devaftation of foreign countries would

would be the pledge of their re-union. In a letter which I faw by accident, *Briffot* wrote as follows, toward the end of laft year, to one of his military minifters; " We muft " *fet fire to the four corners of Europe*, in " that alone is our fafety. *Dumourier* can- " not fuit us; I always diftrufted him. " *Miranda* is the General for us; he under- " ftands the revolutionary power, he has " courage, lights, &c".

To pillage and plunder either at home or abroad is now the law, the very condition of exiftence for the new world fprung up from the dregs and filth of Paris. Four thoufand five hundred million in affignats infeft the circulation, and they will amount to five thoufand million before the end of the year. Does any one imagine, that the Revolutionifts trouble their heads about their liquidation? No fuch thing; and no fuch liquidation could take place without great prejudice to one of their moft effential pro- jects that of dividing amongft the conquerors the conquered mortgage-lands, and to pro- long the attachment of the people, by ex- empting them from all taxes. Thefe two operations require that a portion of the for- tunes of the *Emigrès*, and of others yet to be be confifcated fhould be divided between the foldiers, and the inferior agents of the Republic. This has been already energetically demanded in the fections, in the clubs, and in the commune of Paris; and the Convention by a late decree has already fettled the firft lots. The remainder of the lands thus ufurped, will ferve for the eftate of the nation, and its produce will form the revenue of the Republic; and it will ftand in the place of taxes, which are no more to be propofed, to an armed and fovereign people.

In the mean time, they will live on new Affignats. The national and revolutionary expences will be defrayed by the *Printer* of this paper money; by calls on the pocket books, by extortionary tribunals, and upon a thoufand or two of millions borrowed by the perfuafion of the *permanent guillotine.*

But how is the public to be relieved from this enormous mafs of circulating paper? One of the fureft and moft expeditious methods is, to pufh it out of the kingdom, to enlarge the wound in order to its cure, and to pump out of foreign countries their gold and filver, by a compulfory exchange for fcraps of brown paper, fcrawled over with the

Cap

Cap of Liberty. Many governments have to reproach themselves for having aſſiſted this Coſmopolitan ſpeculation, by the toleration which they gave, and which ſome ſtill preſiſt in giving to a traffic in aſſignats. It is dear and manifeſt that unleſs the courſe of exchange ſhould be reduced almoſt to nothing, aſſignats will ſerve as a ſpunge, and ſuck up imperceptibly all the ſpecie of Europe.

As Mammon, in Paradiſe Loſt, has his eyes always fixed on the golden pavement of Heaven, the Convention have always their fangs ready to ſeize on the public revenues, and private fortunes in all foreign nations.

Let us reflect on the nature of a War, founded on ſuch motives. Let every one then fairly put the queſtion to himſelf, whether in common prudence, it ought to be carried on by halves; if to talk of peace or compoſition is not blaſphemy againſt civil ſociety, and if to enter into treaty with this hydra, before his heads are cut off, is not to deliver up to the monſter every man of property throughout Europe *.

But

---

* This is by no means an hyperbole. The indolent who read not at all, or who read to miſunderſtand, and then forget what they read, conſider every one who ſhews them their danger, as given to exaggeration. The

But I hear it repeated every day,---" Thefe
" wild and extravagant expedients, will be
" their own deftruction; they overturn the
" public oeconomy, ruin the ftate, and dry
" up all the fources of public wealth".

Ah! what is the public welfare, (I an-
fwer) to an Affembly, not one member of
which is at all refponfible for it; which fees
their country only in *the hall in which they
fit*; which is a faction and not a government! They have but one object of pur-
fuit, and that is to fupport the Revolution;
why fhould we object to them thofe calamities,

ruling doctrine of the Jacobins who govern the Convention is, that all the land is in common, and national
property. This principle is repeated every day, by every
public declaimer in the capital. When it was propofed
to exempt veffels belonging to Amfterdam from feizure,
as the property of Patriots, *Boyer Fonfrède*, one of the
moft powerful chiefs, objected, on this ground—That
the Citizens of Amfterdam, *being in eafy circumftances*,
they could not be confidered as *Sans Cullottes*; that the
Sans Cullottes did not fit out 'any fhips, and that the
Sans Cullottes alone were worthy of favour.

Clavierre, the moft wicked and moft artful of thefe
deftroyers, who was Minifter laft October, *did at that
time propofe* to Gen. Montefqueiou, to employ the army
of the Var to extort from the Genoefe a forced loan of
thirty millions in fpecie at four per cent. and to perform
a fimilar operation, by the army of the Alps, on the
States of Berne and Geneva.

mities, in which they find their refources, or the ravages, which furnifh them materials to make props for anarchy?

A year, however, has nearly elapfed in the midft of battles, and as yet there is not the leaft diminution in the refiftance. The houfe is indeed fomewhat fhattered by the violence of the fhocks, but the columns, though tottering, ftill remain on their pedeftals. Not one fortified town has voluntarily opened its gates; not a regiment has abandoned its colours; not an army gives up the field of battle, without *difputing* it moft obftinately; the fhouts of royalty have not yet paffed the lower Loire; fanaticifm nourifhes itfelf on calamities; foldiers die, others take their place; there is no appearance of terror, of wearinefs, or of the leaft return to the better way of thinking.

Such are the difcourfes which, paffing from the talk of private company find their way to camps, and from camps into the cabinets of princes. Their influence produces effects too ftrongly marked, not to make it worth our while to examine the caufes of fuch unconquerable refiftance.

I   Thefe

These causes may all be detailed in a single line. This phænomenon arises chiefly *from that inattention, which did not foresee*, that the resources of a Revolution, necessarily exceed those of mere common War.

One instantly perceives, that besides those means which all the powers have in common, such as, cannon, soldiers, and money, or something which answers as money, the Convention at Paris has ranged under its orders, and with a skill equal to its fruitfulness, all the delusion of opinion, the energy springing from enthusiasm, the fascinating powers of the pen and of the tongue; the passions which have the strongest action in the human breast, the cupidity of command, and the dislike of obedience; interest and vanity; the love of flattery and of respect, the habit of independence, and the certainty of impunity.

It is by alternately availing themselves of these prime movers, that usurpers, without fortune, without extraordinary talents, and exciting horror and disgust by their crimes, have been able to summon to their defence such bodies of blind profligates, and furious fools. *It is thus that,* though abandoned by

its

its firſt proſelytes, ſurrounded by ruin and
misfortune, and attacked by the principal
powers of Europe, the Revolution ſtands
erect, in its bath of blood.

No deſpotic prince could have had authority ſufficient to ſupport the baniſhment of
ſpecie, and the manufacture of Aſſignats.
But the Convention has at this day eſtabliſhed
the currency of its paper upon neceſſity.
The depreciation of this paper muſt ſoon
lead to a cataſtrophe, by the immoderate
price, to which all articles of conſump-
tion muſt be raiſed; but we may ſee that
already, the Revolutioniſts think of turning
ſuch an end to their benefit, by giving up
the landed property to general pillage.

However it may be hereafter, it is evident
for the preſent, that he who maintains the
War with ſpecie, is much weaker in that
reſpect, than he is, who carries it on with
a paper money, the quantity of which has no
limit but his own pleaſure.

Nor is the advantage leſs both for attack
and defence, which ariſes from the univer-
ſal inliſtment of the inhabitants, whoſe fanataciſm and whoſe wants have tied their fate

to

to that of the Revolution, over regular armies brought two or three hundred leagues from their homes, with the immenfe apparatus and train by which they are attended with whom any confiderable misfortune would be nearly romedilefs, and whofe leaders cannot truft any thing to chance, nor act upon contingencies, not forefeen in their inftructions.

When the Convention made that decree, worthy of Xerxes, by which was ordered an immediate and extraordinary levy of three hundred thoufand men, we laughed contemptuoufly, and were juftified in that contempt by reafon. However, this fubfidiary army was to a great degree actually embodied, in the midft of ineffectual murmurs and impotent difcontents.

In addition to ten armies on the Frontiers, we fee a new one fprung up in the revolted Provinces, one of of Royalifts in the Weft, and one under the orders of the Convention in the interior.

Thefe natural forces, and this building of paper, which ftands on a volcano, would neverthelefs, have funk under the weight of difficulties, were it not for the perfeverance of the leaders, in feconding the

moral

moral caufes of their dominion. The moft terrible War which they wage againft their enemies confifts in this; that they oppofe moft extravagant fentiments, to meafures which tend to make them ftill more wildly extravagant.

The events, for two years paft, have enabled thom to deliver the people from all dread of Foreigners. It was much eafier to let this powerful fpring run down, than it is now to wind it up again.

When the nation faw foreign Governments treated with the moft unbounded and contemptuous infolence in the Affembly, in the Clubs, and in millions of writings, with the moft perfect impunity; when it faw that a legiflative affembly was endured, where fovereigns by name, for two years together, received the moft cruel and outrageous affronts; when troops of regicides openly embodied and difciplined, did not draw a fingle foldier from his barracks in any country of Europe; when it was clearly feen that French newfpapers were become the fole arbiters of peace and war, and that they had caught all the powers now waging war quite unprovided, to begin with the Emperor and England, and ending with the Prince of Deux-Ponts; when they

faw

faw the firft campaign clofe with the moft unexpected and rapid conquefts and that after the lofs of thefe conquefts, three months were wafted before the Frontier was even attempted to be attacked; when all this was feen, the people loft not dread only, but even the flighteft refpect for the foreign armies.

The Convention and the Clubs carefully nourifhed thefe difpofitions. It is a fact beyond contradiction, that for ten months paft, not a Royalift has conceived the fmalleft hope, nor a Republican the flighteft alarm from the War.

A camp or two carried; two or three towns taken, have done little to leffen this fecurity. Former experience has made thefe loffes to be confidered as of little confequence; this, and the time which has hitherto conftantly been fpent between every fuccefs of the enemy, and any preffing and vigorous operation by them, have been fo many caufes of allaying their terrors, and lulling reflection to fleep, and thus confirming that confidence by which they are infpired. They know little of the people, of a people in the poffeffion of the fovereignty, and above all, of the people of Paris, who think they can

be

be intimidated by armies waging war, at an hundred leagues diſtance! Out their own circumference, eſpecially in the heart of the kingdom, the exiſtence of ſuch a war is hardly credited. Neither the Convention, nor the Clubs, nor the Coffee-houſes, nor even the Populace have thought them worth their notice, for theſe three months paſt. Intereſt in the War does not paſs beyond the bounds of the office of the Miniſter immediately charged with it; and if the factions at all turn their eyes to the Frontier, it is merely to diſmiſs from their commands, and to hang thoſe Generals, into whoſe places, this or that cabal wiſh to thruſt their own creatures.

The Coalition of the foreign powers has become general, merely by the hoſtilities of the Republic affecting one after the other; the acceſſions to this Coalition being gradual and ſucceſſive, have but ſlighty affected thoſe, who would have been diſmayed and thunderſtruck, by the rapid and unanimous riſing of all Europe. The number of their enemies has become habitual to their thoughts. After having ſeen thoſe enemies one after another floating and undivided, and for a long time uſing the managements of neutrality with the Revolution, a perſuaſion prevailed, that the

league

league of the coalefced powers was not formed on a common intereft, or a uniform principle; and that this forced union would have
no folidity.

This opinion had fhot its roots very deep.
The popular opinion, that there was a project for the difmemberment of France; the
indifference fhown for the fate of the houfe
of Bourbon, and the almoft immediate mixture of negotiation with the operations of
War, has greatly ftrengthened that opinion.
Perfuaded that this league of all the European
powers, had interefts and views quite diftinct
from the re-eftablifhment of the monarchy,
thofe by whom that monarchy was fubverted,
have placed their tactic in the appearance of
a fixed confidence, which would prefently
lead them to a peace.

A joint declaration of the Allied Powers,
which, whilft it would have proved the
unity of their intentions, would have made
their object with its extent manifeft, might
perhaps have weakened thofe delufions; undeceived thofe of all parties who dealt in exag-
gerations, afforded a point round which might
rally all yet undetermined to refift, and fhew
to the fupporters of the prefent confufions,
in a clear light, their inevitable fituation.

But

But thefe are not, by many, all the caufes which to this moment have rendered the War ineffectual againft the Revolution.

Let a juft eftimate be made of the energetic force which its defenders derive from the ties of a common country by which they are bound together; from that great council which has united in itfelf all the powers of the ftate, and contains in it, the hotteft heads, and the moft wicked hearts; which debates and decides in the prefence of the mob; which dogmatizes and decrees, and is at once the inftructor and legiflator of the nation.

Let us attend to the prodigious effect of the clubs; thofe fenates, who have a common center, with the national fenate, who fpread every where its fury, its character, and its decifions, and ferve it as arms to embrace and gather to it the public opinion.

The ravages of the prefs, which keep mens minds in convulfive agitations, and which raife a burning rampart between truth and the people.

Popular doctrines, delivered by ambulatory orators, who enflame or allay enthu-

K   fiafm,

fiafm, who obtain facrifices even from thofe
who appear to have nothing to offer up;
who read lectures upon the declamations,
the monitories, the proclamations of the
affembly, and keep up that conftitutional
fever, the fits of which produce at will,
now a maffacre, now an army.

The ferment raifed in the imagination,
by folemn feafts, whofe atrocious buffoon-
ries can be exceeded by nothing but the
effect they produce, and thofe cannibal fongs
to whofe tunes, *Dumourier* led on to battle and to victory thofe battalions almoft
torn to pieces by the batteries of Gemmappe.

Think what may be effected by Atheifts
vomited out by the fcum of fociety, and
Lords of fuch an empire as France, peo-
pling, at their pleafure, the ftreets with
affaffins, our fire fides with informers; with
one hand opening the prifons, and with the
other, the coffers of the ftate; no longer
putting any bounds to rewards or to punifhments; fquandering men and money as the
duft; oppofing to the calm combination of
their enemies, a ceafelefs ardor, an attention indefatigable to profit by the flighteft
circumftances, and a tenacity of prepoffeffion
which

which does not allow one hour of relaxation, or cool reflexion.

Obferve well the effect of that artificial courage, which never betrays a moment of fear nor indecifion, nor even of doubt of the public fafety; which declares War against Spain, the very day after they had declared War againft Great Britain; which determines the irrefolute, intimidates the difcontented, draws to it the enthufiafts, whilft there is no port affured either within or without, for any penitent Revolutionift, who may refufe to affift in the working of the fhip.

It is no longer a feafon for diffimulation! Why fhould we be furprized at the refiftance which is found, when we place in our view, by the fide of fuch an ufe of times and things, of fentiment and of conjunctures, an unimpaffioned War; a War flow and progreffive, in the midft of events always unforefeen and unthought of; a War which will not employ the moral refources; a circumftantial War of detail, which will be conducted by wifdom and valour, with fcientific ability, but without the leaft reference to the perpetual viciffitudes in the internal ftate of the kingdom?

K 2   SECTION

SECTION V.

Other Causes of Resistance, flowing from the Spirit of the Revolution.

AFTER having pointed out the principles resulting from the nature itself of the War, which weaken its efficacy; after having shewn the probability, that it will neither inspire the factious with terror, nor the Royalists with confidence; nor hold out any hope of security to that immense multitude of undeceived middle men who look for a deliverer; it remains for us to develope the causes drawn from the nature of the Revolution, which concur in producing the same effects.

But this picture, would be the history of four years, and cannot be finished in a few leaves; I must therefore confine myself merely to make a sketch of some of its features.

The minds of men are attached to the existing subversion by two kinds of bands. Some are attached by local or personal interests, interefts, or by the interefts of fome clafs of individuals. The others, with more enlarged views, by the public fpirit which has produced the Revolution. If, inftead of conciliating fome of thefe interefts or feelings; if, inftead of fetting them to fight each other, the attack is made upon them both conjoined, can one be furprized at the obftinacy of their unanimous oppofition?

To give an inftance;---the revolutionary armies confift of three defcriptions of men: of the National Guards who are ftationary, and who have an intereft in the return of peace and good order; the Volunteers, whofe licentious diffolutenefs, requires anarchy, war and rapine; and of the Troops of the Line, who are tied to their condition by duty and by neceffity.

As to the Volunteers, they will remain devoted to anarchy, to the very laft extremity, as to the protector of their debaucheries. To them, all kind of regulation is horrible. It was at them that *Cuftine*, fuch as *Cuftine* is, found himfelf compelled to point a fpecial criminal law, againft *Rapes*. We fhould deceive ourfelves in at all hoping to bring them under any mode of
                                                    fubordination,

fubordination, either by any fenfe of glory,
or of gratitude. The experiment made by
Dumourier, leaves this no longer matter
of opinion, but of certainty.

Affuredly, neither the domeftic national
guards, nor the troops of the line, have
the fame motives to fpill their blood for the
mifcreants whom they ferve. Equity obliges
me to fay, that during the incurfions of the
laft autumn and winter, far from permit-
ting, the foldiers of the line have often repreffed and punifhed outrage and robbery.
A great number of officers, even of the
new creation, deteft the Republic. But
how fhall thefe regiments get loofe from it?
They muft continue in its fervice, under
pain of death; for if they abandon it, all
avenues of efcape are barred againft them.
They are placed between infamy and indi-
gence. At home they are offered honours,
diftinctions and rewards; abroad, utter ruin
and wretchednefs. I might add to this, that
there yet remains a leaven of honour in the
French foldiery, amidft the licentious opinions by which their military principles have
been perverted, which urges them on to
the attack of an enemy who is a foreigner,
and as long as they are kept in ignorance
of

of the determinate object of the hoftility. The influence of this fentiment will not be difputed, when it is recollected that in the War in *La Vendeè*, the troops of the line have frequently joined the Royalifts, or have refufed to fight.

Travel through the whole kingdom, and ftudy the character of the oppofition which is given to the *Counter-Revolution*; a word which implying the abfolute re-eftablifhment of whatever has been changed or abolifhed, ought to have been profcribed at leaft by prudence, and which, having become the watch word of fanatacifm, has given more nerve to the Revolution, than the three-coloured cockade.

You will find the holders of *Affignats*, deceived by the happily infignificant menaces of uninformed Royalifts, falfely perfuaded that the bankruptcy of paper money would be fealed, the very day that the fovereignty in the hands of the monarch, fhould refume the guardianfhip of property; and therefore preferring that difafter which leads to their ruin in the courfe of a year or two, to that calamity which would accomplifh it in an inftant.

You

You will find thofe who have got hold of the goods of the church, dreading reftitution without indemnity, unite themfelves to the fears, and the efforts of the Affignat-holders.

Here, whole provinces, to whom the return of the antient government, perpetually called for, to the great misfortune of thofe who demand it without modifications, prefents the frightful fpectre of the *Gabelle* in all its horrors. There, this image connects itfelf with the re-eftablifhment of the *Aides*, an object no lefs of execration than the *Gabelle*. For *Franch-comptè*, the Counter-revolution is but another name for the refurrection of the tenures by *main-morte*.

Obferve afterwards, what impreffions have been generally made on the great majority of the people, by the inftitutions of the firft Affembly. Make fome calculation of the impulfe which the national character has received from the vaft lottery of fortune for the people to game in; promotions without juft pretenfions, fuccefs without talents, deifications after death without any kind merit, and innumerable offices diftributed by the people collectively, and recieved

cieved

ceived by the people individually. Bring
to account that univerfal change which reverf-
ing all fituations, one after the other, has
caufed all authority to fall into the hands or
men of no defcribeable condition; which has
placed the command of armies in the filth of
the fuburbs, Miniftry in the intriguers of
Grub-Street, and the reprefentation of the
people in the hands of affaffins.

Think how much the fudden elevation of
fo many fuccefsful adventurers of the loweft
orders, of functionaries, of electors, of vef-
try men, of public murderers, of the agents
of anarchy, letting the whole kingdom to
pillage, and ufing the Revolution as a ga-
ming-table, muft have univerfally fpread
the fpirit of emulation and avarice. By
every head cut off, two fortunes are made,
that of the affaffin, and that of his employer.

Set its juft value too on that fanatacifm
of vanity fet in a flame by fuccefsful ambition; the perfonal importance felt by each
individual, and the perpetual fhiftings of
power and command.

Afk the porter in the ftreet, who was
formerly fqueezed between the coach wheel
L   and

and the wall, if he is forry that the coach and he who rode in it, are both vanifhed. Afk that crowd of debtors who have cauf- ed their creditors to be affaffinated; afk the troops of abandoned women, whofe *Civifm* to day ftands inftead of virtue; put the queftion to all thofe of ruined fortunes, who re-eftablifh themfelves by rapine; to the multitude who from humilation have paffed to infolence;---afk from all thefe, if a *Saint Bartholomew*, every month, would difguft them with anarchy.

Make an eftimate of the effects of that independence which manifefts itfelf even in occafional revolts againft the Revolution; and thofe of that prefumption, as infinite and incomprehenfible as is eternity, which fets the feal of perfection on every abfurdity; which is blind to all danger; which never even fufpects itfelf fallible, and which would think itfelf difhonoured if it ceafed to be irrational *.

Laftly,

---

* Prefumption has been, and is ftill one of the hinges on which the Revolution turns. I muft allow myfelf to give two or three inftances :—

The collection of papers found in the Iron Clofet in the Thuilliries, and which have been printed; a collec- tion publifhed by impudence or folly, to demonftrate the King's fcrupulous fidelity to the Conftitution, con-

Laſtly, do not deceive yourſelves as to the degree of hatred which even the deſerters from the Revolution bear to every thing that can bring back the antient monarchy, its inſtruments and its accomplices. Do not forget, that though the multitude both in towns and in the country, have

tains a Letter written to the King by a man, formerly in the Navy, of the name of *Rouyer*, who was conſtituted a Legiſlator in 1791, and was a Conſtituting Legiſlator in 1792 ; and always a moſt brutal Jacobin. This gentleman deſires the King to take him for his Miniſter, on the 17th of *March* 1792, and ſays in his Letter—" I have " taken a careful view, and have gone to the bottom of " affairs ; and have foreſeen every thing that may or " can happen. For the execution of my noble plans, " I aſk nothing more than the direction of the powers " and authority with which the laws has entruſted you. " I know the dangers which I am to face. Weakneſs " numbers them up, but genius vanquiſhes them. I " have conſidered all the Courts of Europe, and I am " ſure I ſhall force them all to ſue for peace."

I know not what he was, but a man, called *Naillac*, ſent by the Convention to Genoa, in his Speech to the Doge, on the 26th of *December* laſt, ſaid—" The Re- " public of France will be an example of public perfec- " tion ;—*Humanity* is neareſt and *deareſt to her heart*, and " ſhe does *not refuſe* to aſſociate the neighbouring coun- " tries to her happineſs."——In this ſtile it was that *Genſonnè* ſaid in the Aſſembly, on the 14th of *March*,— " *In a little time, they, who diſdained ſubmiſſion to the* " *ſovereignty of the French nation, will fall on their knees* " *before the ſovereignty of the world.*"

their

their vexations, yet they have alfo their enjoyments. Forget not that the unfkilfulnefs with which the reftoration of the primitive order of government has been offered to them, without change or foftening, hardens the heart againft Royalty, fixes wavering opinions, fnatches from the good the means of opening the eyes of the people, and raifes legions for the fervice of the bafe and profligate.

No fooner had fome rafh and hot-headed people from abroad, fufficiently fenfible to atrocious injuries, but ill informed as to the interefts of their party, pronounced the terrible fentence of " *all or nothing,*" but they taught their enemies the fame warhoops; they taught it even to thofe who had ceafed to be their enemies, and who had nothing held up to them but implacable revenge, or unavailing repentance.

I have before me, one of thofe publications, in which complaints fupply the place of argument, and invective is fubftituted for redrefs *. If the charms of genius and fine writing could reftore the monarchy, this pamphlet would have fulfilled the intentions

of

* Letters upon the Republic of 1793, &c. &c.

of its author. But a defective judgment has
hurried him, unknown to himself, into the
views of the Republicans. Every one would
have liftened attentively to a writer who
had fatisfied himfelf with effacing the fan-
taftic pictures which had been made of the
old government, and with demonftrating that
the old government, though too variable and
arbitrary, became daily lefs abfolute; that the
reign of *Louis XVI.* was a reign of great
moderation and lenity; that in no country
have minifters lefs ventured on acts of high
authority, than in general did the minifters
of this Prince, who was filled with defire
for the public good, with mildnefs, and with
refpect for the laws ; and laftly, had fhewn,
that a fatal want of fteadinefs had enervated
the operations of government; and that
perfonal interefts, or the interefts of claffes
of men, having too often fuccefsfully oppofed authority, this relaxation prepared the
overthrow of all authority. No informed
man would have contefted thefe well-known
truths, which would have placed in the
cleareft light, the abominable nature of the
exifting Revolution.

But whilft the real fault was, that the
monarch did not hold fufficiently faft his
lawful

lawful authority, this author would lead us to believe that his error lay in not ftraining it to abufe; he takes the violent exceffes of government for its refources, and from the depths of his retirement in Germany, he propofes thefe his maxims as the means of pacifying and difarming a nation, whofe efforts balance thofe of all Europe; and whofe fanataciſm is hardly fatisfied by the moſt licentious liberty.

I proteſt, in the name of all true Royaliſts, *, againſt a declaration like this, whofe publication in France would be equivalent to the loſs of two battles; which would make the Revolution immortal, and would oppofe more difficulties, and create more danger to the allied powers than all the Regicide Clubs.

If

* I have fpoken in their name more than ohce, and they have never difavowed me. Though a Foreigner, and born uuder a Republican Government, I have acquired, by four years fpent without any reafonable certainty at going to bed, that I fhould awake to liberty or fo life; at the coft of three arrefts of my perfon, of one hundred and fifteen denunciations, of the feal twice put on my effects and papers, by four *civic* aſſaults on my houfe, and by the confifcation of all my property in France; by thefe, I fay, I have acquired, the rights of a Royaliſt, and as nothing remains for me to gain by this title but the *Guillotine*, I fancy that no one will be tempted to difpute it with me.

If it was neceſſary for the Convention to inflame enthuſiaſm anew, they would in a proclamation give a ſecond edition of the principles of this writer, and copying from him, would ſay to the nation :---

" Expect not any of the advantages which
" this King offers you, whoſe martyrdom
" and whoſe memory, ſeem to have given a
" religious ſanctity to his will and pleaſure.
" To royalty now dead and buried, they
" are about to add every thing that rendered
" it odious to you. Now that you are ma-
" ſters and ſovereigns, will you give up
" your deſtiny to the moſt *abſolute of mo-*
" *narchs?* You have a leaning to the reſto-
" ration of monarchy; think well, that it
" is *eſſentially a feudal Government.* You
" have declared the commons alone to be the
" nation; well then, our adverſaries exclude
" the commons intirely, and teach you that
" the nobility and clergy, are the true and
" original repreſentatives of the nation."

" Louis XVI. your King, recognized your
" right to impoſe taxes, by your States-Ge-
" neral; but you have done much better
" than ſettling the right of taxation, for
" you pay no taxes at all. To ſmooth the
                                        " way

" way to your fubmiſſion, they tell you now,
" that the fyſtem of *Louis-le-Grand* ſhall
" alone decide as to taxation; and that the
" will and pleaſure of *Comptrollers-General*,
" ſhall be ſubſtituted for your States-Ge-
" neral.

" All your inſtructions in 1789, called for
" the ſuppreſſion of *Intendants* ; they will
" be again beſtowed on you, as the *Maſter-*
" *ſpring, to give rapid motion to Govern-*
" *ment, and becauſe Monſ. Neckar had*
" *calumniated them.* Enlightened and ho-
" neſt men, would in vain object, by repre-
" ſenting, that in proportion as power is
" concentered in the Prince, the greater is
" the danger of entruſting it to the exerciſe
" of individuals, and to abſolute inſtruments.
" That ſubordinate adminiſtrations, bound
" by fixed rules, and who govern in the
" ſpirit of *routine*, are preferable to Vice-
" roys, who have an inſtinctive and inva-
" riable diſpoſition to make themſelves
" ſtronger than the law, and to ſtrain their
" authority, by introducing an arbitrary
" power, worſe than deſpotiſm itſelf.

" The *Letters de Cachet* were our com-
" mon topic of perſuaſion to make you take
" arms

" arms againſt Royalty, and by your una-
" nimous deſire, they were proſcribed;
" they will be reſtored to you as the *means*
" *of correction.* Acts of arbitrary power will
" again make their appearance, as ſo many
" *favours.* You have deſtroyed the *Baſtille*,
" and they will build many of them for
" you, and on a larger ſcale. Juſtice, love
" for his people, the deſire to do good, ſim-
" plicity of manners, will be forbidden to
" the King, as *falſe principles of popularity.*
" Not one of our new improvements will
" be preſerved, not one abuſe condemned.
" Make now then your election between
" the independence which you have ob-
" tained by conqueſt, and the moſt un-
" meaſured and unlimited ſubjection."

At theſe words, all their diſſentions will
vaniſh, the camps will again be filled, rage
and deſpair will have their conſummation in
freſh maſſacres, the Convention will regain
its credit, and the Royaliſts will loſe theirs.

Theſe are the rocks, on which, for four
years, they have perſiſted to drive us, by
theſe declamations which favour of a Turkiſh
Divan, and which are the cauſe of all the
calumnies by which the Princes, brothers

of

of Louis XVI. together with their councils, and all the Royalifts are daily blackened; declamations which their utter and affecting impotence, make as ridiculous as ill-judged, and which every where multiply the partifans of the Revolution.

Under this laft confideration, does the anonymous Writer * really think that the Courts to which he addreffes his inftructions with fuch a tone of authority, will be much obliged to him for his revelations? Does he think that they will greatly applaud him for this difference which he proclaims to exift between the interefts of the Sovereign, and the interefts of the people? Does he ferioufly think it to be altogether prudent to exhibit the allied Sovereigns as confpiring to eftablifh defpotifm, at a time, when great occafions command great facrifices, when the general ftaggering of opinions, have fet all the innovators,

---

* The Pamphlet, into the detail of which the Author of this Piece enters fo much at large, was fcarcely worth his notice, as it contains the fentiments of very few, if any, of the Emigrants. At a time like this, the Prefs fwarms with the works of all forts of Speculators; and it is not very furprizing (and hardly worth much obfervation) that fome perfons viewing, with a due horror, the atrocious proceedings which have introduced this Revolution, and attended it in every ftage of its progrefs, fhould be inclined to think the worft abufes of the old Government, a fort of comparative benefits.

novators, the profligate and the enthufiafts in every country, into fearful agitation.

Has he reflected what impreffion his doctrines might make in that renowned ifland, whofe fleets now hide the feas, and whofe legions cover Flanders, where the love of Liberty and Royalty are infeperable ; and whofe government has not the power (happily it has not the defire) to arm the people for the re-eftablifhment of Baftilles.

Is it thus he hopes to determine the motions of the free and warlike confederated Cantons, whofe fons, alone incorruptible in the midft of the vileft corruption, have fpilled their blood at the foot of a fubverted throne; and amongft whom, the perfidious enemies of their peace, have already made the Revolution but too popular ?

Alas! it is high time to put an end to this mode of difgracing a facred caufe, by unceafingly demanding the facrifice of all Liberty. Whilft Kings and people breathe one common wifh for the eftablifhment of a limited and lenient Government, let thofe who difapprove be filent ; for though their clamours fhould be loft in the clouds, yet will they tend to increafe the tempeft by which we are toffed.

M 2   SECTION

SECTION VI.

A comparative State of France in the last Spring, and at this Instant. Vicissitudes in its Anarchy.

IF, after an analysis, unfortunately too faithful, of *the destiny which governs the* Revolution; of its ultimate object and of its resources; if after this we should add, that at no period of its existence, has it been in such manifest danger, this opinion would have the air of a paradox; but it will ceafe to be such with those, who not suffering themselves to be dazzled by chimerical hopes, nor subdued by exaggerated fears, will weigh the resources of the Convention with those she furnishes to her enemies.

I say the Convention, because it is the very soul of the Revolution. It is to no purpose to attack the one, whilst the other has existence. Battles and sieges; all the stuff of gazzettes by which idlenefs is amused, are entirely thrown away as long as new fortifications and new armies can be derived from the center. A few scratches on the foot,

foot, do not prevent the heart from renew-
ing the circulation of the blood.

Againſt whom is it that confederated
Europe has now for ſix months, made a
war by attacking the Frontiers? Upon an
enemy, againſt whom the half of ſubjugated
France calls for avengers; againſt a committee of *Neros* taken from the dregs of
the people, who are now become objeᶜts of
horror to their firſt accomplices, and the
cut-throats of all amongſt themſelves, who
make an halt in the march of wickedneſs;
whoſe boundleſs tyranny furniſhes a proof
of the extent and the magnitude of the
public diſcontents; with the moſt hardened
effrontery breaking through laws made by
themſelves; forcing all deſcriptions of in-
tereſts to riſe againſt them, paſſing from
maſſacres to formal executions, and returning from executions to maſſacres; impri-
ſoning without attention even to forms;
putting to death upon the ſlighteſt ſuſpicion;
gagging all mouths with their charter of the
Rights of Man; oppreſſing ſpeech, the preſs,
and even thought itſelf; violating the domeſtic aſylum; opening letters; carrying
terror and conſternation into every family;
Atheiſts who have proclaimed that GOD
was

was a *miscreant* whom Hell itself would have trembled at receiving; and, in a word now reigning over none but the victims which they have made, or those whom they reserve for future sacrifice.

No ability or talents whatsoever at this time support this Junto. I thas reduced the art of Government to corruption and assassination. It is by terror that they chain down *a free people*; but, going far beyond the most frantic tyrants, they prepare for themselves the fate of tyrants.

By extending their oppression to all the parties, their own excepted, who had embraced the cause of the Revolution, they have made its destruction an object of the wishes of those who were originally most devoted to it. Covered over with horror and contempt, the turpitude of the Convention has enfeebled it, as much as its butcheries. Public opinion supported the former assemblies, but this is obliged to support opinion. No longer defended by principles, which have been betrayed by its practices, the hypocrisy of the Convention, cannot screen its abominations.

The

The Convention is now in its progrefs from the Republican Revolution, to that laſt anarchic Revolution which I have deſcribed; and ſhe muſt perfect it, or periſh. But to arrive at that *perfection*, in the midſt of a war which preſſes her on every ſide, ſhe is compelled to ſtrain to its height every ſpring, and by daily uſe, their elaſticity is ſlackened.

Compare their reſources, at this day, with thoſe of laſt year, and the compariſon is to their diſadvantage. There is no miſtaking a remarkable change which has taken place in the reſpective belligerent powers. In ſpite of her juggling tricks, her decrees and her prodigality, the Convention has not been able to embody more than three hundred four thouſand men, for her defence both abroad and at home. A fourth part, and more of this force is employed in garriſons. The ſieges and the capture of Condè, of Mayence and Valenciennes, have weakened her force by thirty five thouſand men. She has to combat againſt nearly four hundred thouſand, and ſhe has a civil war in the heart of the kingdom. Her flag has diſappeared; and ſhe has abandoned the ſea, her foreign ſupply
ply

ply of provifions and her commerce, to
the fleets of her enemies.

She has got rid in fucceffion of the few
general officers, whofe military talents were
her protection. In the fpace of fix months
twenty three of them have been accufed,
difgraced and difmiffed. Four have died
a violent death, two upon the fcaffold, and
twelve have fled their country *. The fate
of the French arms is then, at this day
entrufted to the mere refufe of their military.

The gulph of peculation and of the public expenditure, fwallows up every month
a fum greatly fuperior to the annual revenue
of the moft opulent monarchy. The depreciation of *Affignats* is the thermometer to
afcertain the decline of the Convention.
The price of all commodities rifing every
day

---

* This number will certainly be augmented, whilft
this work is at the prefs. If any thing more than another proves the general madnefs, it is this fucceffion of
inefficient Commanders, who, from the example of their
predeceffors, are certain, on the firft fufpicion, on the
firft misfortune, to pafs from favour to difgrace ; from
the fword of the enemy, to the dagger of the affaffin ;
from their camp to the fcaffold; yet proudly undertake
to fupport the power of their future executioners.

day moſt exorbitantly, government, the principal conſumer, ſuſtains a loſs equal to the expences of a whole Campaign. In a little time the people will be no longer able to procure ſubſiſtence; and to get over this deſperate criſis, the Jacobins will deliver the fruits of the earth, the earnings of induſtry, the purſes and, the pocket books, to the pillage of the multitude. Nothing ſhort of a deadly torpor within the kingdom, and in the foreign forces, can ſave the Revolution from being buried in the ruins of ſuch an earthquake.

Already deſpair has gained ſome over, and depreſſion has affected others. Conſternation is every where; rage has changed its object, and fanataciſm whets the poniard of the oppreſſed, as well as that of the oppreſſor.

This formidable revolutionary Confederacy has let in the light upon itſelf; it has ſhewn its very inwards in all their nakedneſs; it was Pandora's box, and Hope has taken its flight out of it. If almoſt every confederacy is faulty by a want of union and and concert; if the uſe of their means is rarely correſpondent to their extent; if unforeſeen diſputes and incidental diſſen-

N   tions

tions weaken their combination,---what muſt we expeđ from diſcordant factions, diſputing with one another for exiſtence and empire, in a country turned upſide down, where the ruling party itſelf has no other means of holding the reins of government, but a choice of violences.

Like to Saturn, the Revolution devours its children. The formidable conjunction which bound all its parties together and directed their motions, is now diſſolved. The Convention and its Clubs ſtrenuouſly endeavour to concenter them in their boſom; but, before they can aecompliſh this, the revolted cities and departments muſt be reduced; the victorious Royaliſts in the Weſt muſt be ſubdued; ſyſtematic combinations muſt be prevented; the dangerous example of effectual reſiſtance muſt be effaced.

Nevertheleſs, we muſt not diſguiſe it from ourſelves that in theſe interior diviſions the probabilities are ſtill in favour of the Convention; its title alone gives the ſanction of law to its meaſures; ſhe obtains obedience from the habits of obeying; tribunals, aſſignats, the favours, and the ſeductions of unlimited power are all in her diſpoſal.

difpofal. Under her orders alfo acts that fanguinary corporation of Jacobins, whofe invifible powers prepare fecret dangers, put the refolutions of confpiracy in execution, raife or appeafe an infurrection, pierce into the moft hidden retreats, and are the efficient agents of the revolutionary power *.

For

* This Corporation is not a being of the fancy. The actors in infurrections, in conflagrations, in maffacres, really form a confraternity. Syftematically organized, they have their catechifm, their *flang*, their colonels, their majors, their captains; their profeffion and their noviciate; their points of correfpondence, their refpective tafks, their departments, their cuftoms, and the laws of their order. Even in foreign countries this infernal fociety has its *affiliated* Clubs; it has excited all the mafter crimes of the Revolution; and has attempted, in twenty parts of Europe, commotions fimilar to thofe which it has raifed in France. It had its origin in the *Palais-royal*, and has been the right-hand of the leading confpirators. *Rotondo Fournier*, an American, *Eftienne*, formerly a captain of the *Sans Cullottes*, at Bruffels; *L'Huillier*, *Procureur-General* of the department of Paris; *Maillard*, formerly a bum-bailiff; the leading men of the Club of the *Cordeliers*, have been the principal Officers in this Regiment. M. *de la Fayette* knew it and dreaded it; but never had the courage to attack it in earneft. The laft enterprize plotted by *Rotondo*, was againft Geneva, where he has been arrefted fome months fince. I could add fome moft extraordinary details to thefe few lines; but I confine myfelf to merely affuring the Public, that they have as yet, but a very fuperficial knowledge of the Revolution in its prefent

For want of exact and comparative information, it is difficult to form a positive judgment on the troubles which exist in the interior of the kingdom. But, through all uncertainties, and by the help of what we have already seen, one may perceive that, for want of concert between the commotions within the kingdom, and the operations from without, the force which menaced the Convention, has not as yet essentially affected its authority.

Several of the departments in *Rebellion,* have submitted. The Convention has subdued them by their own *Municipalities,* to which they had dictated intentions adverse to those of their *Directories;* just as when the occasion calls for it, they can raise the *Sections* against the refractory Municipalities. The first attempts of *Wimpfen* in Normandy, ended in his retreat before a *Quack,* one *Seyffert,* who formerly distributed his pills at the *Palais Royal,* and who is now a general in the army. By the small body of troops under the command of this Quack,

you

state, and that one cannot too much lament the improvidence of those, who think they sufficiently secure themselves against it, by raising some walls about its territories.

you may form an eſtimate of the weakneſs of the inſurgents of Calvados, and every
thing leads us to believe, that, ſome unforeſeen events excepted, the inſurgents will
be moſt fortunate, if they can maintain their
independence in Lower Normandy.

The coalitions in the South have ſhewn
more of vigour, of ſyſtem and of reſources.
Lyons and *Marſeilles* had the addreſs, to
adopt the arms of their adverſaries. To
revolutionary tribunals, they oppoſed anti-
revolutionary tribunals; clubs of worthy
men, to clubs of cut-throats; aſſociations
of men of property to thoſe of bare-breeched
robbers ; manly and vigorous addreſſes to the
waſte paper of Paris; active reſiſtance
againſt oppreſſion, to inſurrections, and the
moſt hateful tyranny; and their proclamation of independence, to the authority of
the Convention.

Theſe cities had the wiſdom to make
their advances by degrees and with great
caution, until their combination was more
general and conſolidated. They took care
not to erect the ſtandard of Royalty all at
once, leſt they might make the Republicans and the *Maratiſts* rally their forces;
                                          and

and they chofe reftoration of order as the
road to political re-eftablifhment. Already
had their plan been attended with fuccefs.
Eighteen thoufand Royalifts were in arms
at Lyons, and Marfeilles had fent them
fuccours. But the total inactivity of the
Sardinian Auftrian troops, left a free courfe
to a part of Kellerman's army. Thefe,
ufelefs in Savoy, the allies not having paffed
the Alps, were directed againft Lyons;
another divifion of that army cut off the
paffage of the Marfellians, and thus this
important diverfion, the confequence of
which might have been the lofs of the whole
South of France to the Convention, is on
the eve of difappearing intirely.

It is plainly to be feen, that this approach-
ing misfortune, will affect the Royalifts in
La Vendèe. The Convention, difembarraffed
of the other internal revolts, will re-unite
all its forces againft the *Lower Loire*. If
the army of the Royalifts, notwithftanding
its brilliant and long fuftained advantages,
has not as yet been able for more than a
moment, to extend itfelf on the right of
that River; if the towns which they took
have been evacuated; if they have not got
poffeffion of a fingle fea-port, nor the accef-
fion

fion of one important city, nor the junc-
tion of any of the furrounding departments,
as the confequence of their many victories;
if the fruit of thefe victories, has been, to
this inftant, no other than their preferving
the contefted diftinct;---does it not refult
from all this, that the forces are nearly
balanced, that their fituation is ftill preca-
rious, and that there can be no decided
opinion formed as to the further progrefs
of the Royalifts?

It requires no great forefight to perceive
that this momentary equilibrium will be
foon deftroyed, either in favour of the
monarchy, if the cities in the South fhould
rife in refiftance to the dangers which threa-
ten them, and act in concert with the *Lower
Loire*; or, in favor of the Convention, if
the external war does not change its character; and if, having loft all hope of
fpeedy fuccour, the infurgents of the South
in Normandy and Brittany, with thofe
which dare not yet fhew themfelves, are
fubdued by the ufurpers, or forced to capi-
tulate on terms of accomodation.

Value, as you chufe, thefe refpective
chances, one or other of thefe events muft
happen

happen before winter. Let the *Jacobins* triumph, they will acquire the fame authority which the *Republicans* poffeffed laft year. Their caprices and villainies will enjoy the fame afcendant; the foreign war will fee its influence decreafed; a laft effort of anarchy will confirm the reign of *Sans-Cullotifm*, and I much doubt whether the lofs of fix Frontier towns will contribute materially to fhake it from the Throne.

SECTION

SECTION VII.

Conclusion. Auxiliary Measures of the War. Misconception of the French in the Interior, as to the Motives of the War. The mistaken Opinions entertained Abroad, of the general disposition of Mens Minds in France.

EXAMINING the history of all wars which have been caused by a great agitation of opinions, we see that opposed opinions have resisted many victories, when the conqueror has neglected to give a proper direction to the public mind. The defeats of the Lutherans, the Hussites and the Calvinists, did not destroy the Protestant religion. A cotemporary writer has ingeniously observed, that never did a General find recruits for his army amongst authors; but that very often the authors found recruits amongst the soldiers. All Revolutions present us with a mixture of enthusiasm, wickedness, and weakness. In a warfare with them, the necessary skill consists in undeceiving the enthusiasts; subjugating the wicked, and effeciently protecting the weak. Accordingly, when a new doctrine has laid hold of the minds of men,

O   we

we fhould by no means think of oppofing it
by force alone; for never were opinions killed
by cannon balls. Thefe may flaughter the
impoftors, the knaves, the banditti who
drag the multitude into mifchievous ways
of thinking; but the method of giving
them the fuperiority, or of giving them
new life, would be, on one hand, to leave
them unpunifhed; and, on the other, to
attempt totally to immolate with them,
the opinions which they have perverted,
which will furvive them, and the immediate repreffion of which would, by its
principle, deftroy that moral dominion,
without which it is now impoffible to govern
mankind.

We muft leave, then, to gafconading
politicians, the idea, that the kingdom can
be fubdued by force alone. The fubmiffion
which is poffible, which ought moft ear-
neftly to be prayed for; the fubmiffion,
which by deftroying the very foundations of
a ferocious anarchy, would prevent new
Revolutions, will never refult from other
means, than *force* and *perfuafion* united.

Without this union, the war will indeed
be fufficient to harrafs the kingdom, but
not

not to fubdue it. It will exhauft the prefent refources of the Convention, but it will
furnifh it with the means of finding new
refources. If it fhould tear the country
internally to pieces, it muft end in fubdivi-
fions of the Republic, in which the trade,
the creditors of France, and the balance of
power throughout Europe will find their
grave; whilft the ifolated ftate of that
country, offering it as an eafy prey to its
neighbours, prepares for us half a century
of wars, and of taxes.

Every one perceives that force may be
made the firft ftep to perfuafion, provided
that it keeps mens minds in unremitting
alarm, that it acquires dominion over mens
hopes, and that by a rapid activity, it leaves
no time for fear to fubfide, or repentance to waver. It is for Cabinets and
for Generals then to determine the quality
of military operations. It would be imper-
tinent to prefs further a truth, which cannot have efcaped their penetration.

But, the ignorance of its final object, is
the greateft obftacle to the dominion of
force, as intended to influence opinion.
The defigns, then, of the Allied Powers

being

being quite mysterious (I say it now a second time) their enemies find in their silence
an inexhaustible source of resistance. It
serves them as the means of nourishing
prejudices, of continuing popular delusion,
to found the public wildness upon a principle, and successfully to ballance the terror
of the Allied Armies, with the dread of the
consequences which would flow from their
progress in the kingdom.

These secret proceedings do not impose
solely on the mere people, or on those
in arms; they have also their influence, and
that a very strong influence, on the greater part
of the partisans of a monarchical government,
all of whom are attached to the preservation
of the kingdom entire, and of whom the
majority are as averse from an arbitrary, as
from a foreign master.

Whatever may be the intentions of the
Allied Powers in regard to France, no per-
son of understanding can give credit to the
absurd report, of an indefinite dismember-
ment, the execution of which would prolong the war for many years, and in its
consequences beget many new wars. It
is an injurious calumny which confounds
with

with a fyftematic intention of keeping what
is got, fome conquefts inevitable in the fortune of war, indemnities for enormous expences, which are ufeful more as means of
fecurity, than as objects of aggrandifement,
and which may all be fettled and limited according to circumftances, by definitive treaty.

But though thinking men reject thefe exaggerated diftrufts, they however lay hold of
the vulgar mind. The chiefs of the Revolution hold out to the French, the example
of Poland, they prophecy for them a fimilar
deftiny. Thefe forced inferences inftil fears
into the neutral powers of the fecond order,
and they fhew the Royalifts in the interior
of the kingdom, in the light of faithlefs citizens, fighting againft the independence of
their country.

To this firft obftacle to converfions, is added
another, and not lefs effectual; and which
grows from the fame caufe. It is an opinion univerfally entertained in the kingdom,
and too many violent difcourfes have ftrengthened it, that the powers have leagued together for the eftablifhment of defpotifm; that,
after having effected an unqualified counter-
revolution by force of arms, they will maintain

tain it by the gallows, and that they will plunge again into flavery, a nation already moft feverely punifhed by their miftake, as to the nature of true liberty.

How fhall the people, the troops, the whole nation get the better of thefe prejudices, as long as they fhall remain between falfe *friends,* who perpetuate their credulity, and *enemies* who will not condefcend to undeceive them? And yet we are filled with indignation by the duration of the public mifconduct! and we are quite at a lofs how to account for a refiftance, the food for which we ourfelves abundantly furnifh!

Alas! when we affume the government of men, we ought to take the trouble of ftudying the human heart, to give a direction to its inclinations, and to enlighten it in its decifions.

If I was allowed to look into thofe councils, in which the fate of Europe is difcuffed, I fhould find, perhaps, that too little confidence was placed in the effect of a public Manifefto, which might fhew to the French nation, and to all nations, the reafons which make the exifting war, a true and real war for civilized fociety.

It

It has been too often, and too foolishly said, that the present was the cause of kings. This prattle of the Anti-chamber, has passed from the mouths of courtiers, into the mouths of the anarchists. It is needless to ask the latter, if such discourse does or does not tend to draw the popular favour to their interests, by making them the common interests of every people, and by holding them out as in opposition to the interests of sovereigns.

I say aloud, and boldly, if the business stood thus, the Revolution would be immortal; but it will perish, for it is an outrageous and wicked attack upon the *people of all countries,* still more than on their governments, it is much more of a conspiracy against the *rights of nations,* than in favour of the *rights of men.*

Why will not then the Allied Powers prove this important truth, by demonstrating to people of France that their prosperity, inseparable from that of Europe, makes the war a matter of necessity, and not of choice?

That the indisputable right of every independent nation, that of reforming its own
laws,

laws, a right which no state difputes with the French, cannot extend to offending againft the rights of the people in every nation, or give a legal fanction to rapine and murder.

That no political fociety can fuffer clofe to her, a *Revolutinary* power, which makes laws to day, in order to reverfe them tomorrow; which fubverts the principle of all agreement amongft men; which promifes abroad, what it has executed at home, to deliver all property to its plunderers, and the lives of men to its affaffins.

That no ftate, no fovereign, no people has the prerogative, to attack, by its inftitutions, that order without which civilized fociety connot exift, and which is indifpenfibly neceffary to univerfal juftice.

That all nations are under one general law; that they all have common rights and interefts, and ties; that they are linked together by their defire of mutual fafety and mutual credit; and that all countries guarantee to each other the inviolability of perfon and property.

That

That a fixed and juft government is the moft facred of all properties; that fovereign magiftracies exift only to preferve the focial chain, and that he who firft breaks it, returns into the condition of favages.

That the tyrants, who boafted that they could regenerate the kingdom, have reduced it to this point of degradation, and thereby have excluded France from the law of nations, and all civilized order.

That they have declared war againft all men of landed propeity, by drowning the right of poffeffion in the blood of the proprietor; by rewarding the crimes of their accomplices, at the expence of honeft men; by drying up all the fources not only of riches, but of fubfiftence; by ftriking down at once the colonies and commerce of their country, the fea-ports and the work-fhops; induftry and agriculture, all exchange of produce between France and foreign countries.

That all civil and commercial intercourfe is deftroyed for them, by the boundlefs fabrication of affignats with compulfory currency, that food for fabulous expence, the fraudulent tokens, of an imaginary value, and

P   founded

founded upon fecurities uncertain, contefted and illegal.

That the inevitable depreciation of this money of opinion; the eafy fraud which it prepares towards the creditors of France, the total overthrow which it would effect of all fortunes and of all commerce, have impe-rioufly dictated its prohibition in every country.

That every nation arrived at this perfection of *diftemper*, and fubject to the fanguinary anarchy by which it is perpetuated, no lon-ger makes a part of the general Society. Exifting for no other purpofe but its own ruin and that of all other people, it has made it of indifpenfible neceflity, that it fhould it-felf perifh, or deftroy every thing elfe.

That it is the duty of the Allied Powers to prevent both one and the other of thefe cataftrophes; to deliver France from the horrors of its own anarchy, or to fave Europe from perifhing in the fhipwreck of France.

The protection of families, of the public tranquility, and of property, is the great end and duty of Government; and this unalterable principle ought to unite them all. They are armed to be the guardians of all ranks and conditions

conditions of life, to preserve to the people, their altars; to the laws, their empire; to the rights of all men, their sanctity; and to the public morals, their authority.

That they have united their forces to bring France back to order, to subordination and to safety; the advantages of which have been ravished from them by a licentious faction; and that they will lay down their arms as soon as that wretched country, delivered from the tyranny of crimes, shall return under a government, from which stability and public tranquility may be expected.

Perhaps language of this kind might weigh with that majority, who though detesting the present state of things, are not the less alarmed for the future, and regard the War only as an instrument for forcing their free will, and therefore make resistance still more from ignorance than anger.

Two mistakes have succeeded each other, and both equally dangerous. The same head-long judgment which made all pass for incorrigible *Revolutionists*, who entertained any of the recent opinions, at this day hurries many minds into the false notion, that the
whole

whole kingdom reftored to its fenfes, the furious Republicans excepted, wifh to return precifely to that ftate from which they ftarted.

But let us not deceive ourfelves. The fpirit of the Revolution will be its fucceffor, as it was its precurfor; it has been purified even in the brains of thofe whom it oppreffed. The Jacobins are regarded with horror, and a government is ardently wifhed for, which might annihilate them. Anarchy difgufts and terrifies; but in its viciffitudes, new interefts have been difcovered. It is eafy to fay that thefe particular interefts alone giving ftrength to the Revolution, the moment they are all facrificed, the Revolution will be at an end, and the ftate will be faved. By reafoning fimilar to this, the factious have prepared their own deftruction. In what then does the general intereft confift, if it is not in the harmonious concord of individual interefts? what oppofition muft you not expect, if you found a new order of things, be that order what it may, upon grief and defpair?

To effect a counter-revolution, which will require fupport is not the whole of what we have to do. But to effect and to
consolidate

confolidate it, fuch a force, as we have not, or perfuafion which would be inefficacious without that force, or the union of one and of the other is abfolutely neceffary.

There was, perhaps, in the laft year, a moment of time, when terror might have deftroyed the principle of all refiftance, and removed all difficulties from the future. But this moment is paffed. Now, the utter defolation of the kingdom, has divided the Revolution into four or five diftinct parties. If all alliance, if every kind of compofition, if all management with this mercilefs crew who reign over Paris and the monarchy, the bloody dagger always in hand, is be-come impoffible, may we not perceive a principle which will foon unite thefe parties under one ftandard, in the neceffity by which their enemies in the interior of the kingdom are impelled to their deftruction? We may affure ourfelves, beyond all doubt, that all will feek peace, fecurity and liberty under the protecting authority of a monarch, who fhall be powerful enough to give effi-cacy to the laws; but is it equally certain that they will inveft him with a prerogative to infringe the law? Is it to be expected that they intend, or that it is in their power to make
the

the Revolution again and in an inftant, de-
fecend from the top of that ladder of infamy
on which it is now mounted to its loweft
round. Is fuch a tumble in nature, in the
circumftances of affairs, or in the mode of
thinking of the day ?

However this may be, it is eafy to fee
through all this, that if this combination of
Kings, fhould fucceed in rooting out the Republicans, it will give the law, and that irre-
fiftibly; that whatever political arrangements
it may propofe, they will be no other than the
award of an arbritration, the terms of a detailed treaty between the crown, and the parties who fhall have replaced it on the head of
the Bourbons.

But we cannot entertain even an hope that
fuch an ending as this, will fatisfy all mens
wifhes, will arrange all the elafhing fyftems,
will conciliate all interefts, or, in a word,
that it will guarantee to the Monarchy a ftate
exempt from factions, and from troubles.
Men governed by their paffions, never fee
more than two poffible fituations, the worft
or the beft. But fentence has been long fince
pronounced on us, that we fhould be fatisfied
with paffing from the extreme of evil, to a
condition fomewhat lefs bad.

The

The eftablifhment of order for the time to come, muft be founded on an exact knowledge of the general difpofitions. When this is rated too high or too low, we daily purchafe bleffings which are given to our hopes, but never delivered to our poffeffion. It is much lefs dangerous to forefee difficulties than to deny them, for, every miftake as to their exiftence, will lay falfe foundations for our beft concerted projects, and will become the caufe of new misfortunes.

Two defpotic fovereigns hover over our wills; neceffity, and the imperious progrefs of human affairs. Whilft the vulgar, like fo many children, meditate on what *ought to be done*, reafon and experience look to what *can be done*. How abfurd to talk continually *of principles*, in affairs which depend intirely upon circumftances. Wifdom, genius and patriotifm endeavour to turn the circumftances to account, and to bend them gently to their ufe, inftead of rafhly flying in their face. Such was the policy of Henry the IV. and of his Minifter. We need not blufh to tread in the fteps of two fuch Leaders.

If high fpirited men, who find reflection a punifhment, and confider moderation as
treafon,

treafon, fhould attribute my opinions to my *fe-cret leanings* to the caufe of Liberty; I tell fuch men, that born under her empire and formed under her tuition, fhe taught me one leffon, which had made a deep impreffion on me, long before the year 1789; it is this, that *France was incapable of fupporting political Liberty, without thirty years of preliminary training.*

It will be eafily believed, I fancy, that the Revolution as not altered my way of thinking; and, as it has difcovered to us that a corrupt people are a thoufand times worfe than ty-rants, I will infcribe on the dreadful monu-ment raifed by their wicked and furious ex-ceffes, a leffon which has, for fifteen years paft, given my thoughts their directon, and which an Englifh Poet has written for us in two lines:

" For Forms of Government let Fools conteft;
" Whate'er is beft adminifter'd is beft."

F I N I S.

I have

I have reduced the Military Force in actual Service, which the Convention oppoſes to its Enemies, to three hundred and four thouſand Men. Take the following diſtribution, which I give you from a careful Review; each Article being put down at the higheſt.

	Men.
Army in the North – – –	30,000
Camp of Magdelaine – –	12,000
Camp of Caſſel – –	12,000
Garriſons in different Parts of Flanders	30,000
At Givet and Sedan – – –	18,000
Army on the Moſelle – – –	30,000
Garriſons on the Meuſe and Lorrain –	25,000
Army of Beaucharnais – – –	30,000
Garriſons in Alſace, and Franche Comté	15,000
Camp at Huningue – – –	16,000
Army of the Alps, and of Var –	60,000
Army of Rouſillon – – –	18,000
Army of Bayonne – – –	12,000
Army of Vendèe – –	
Army of Evreux – – –	4,000
	304,000 *

* Thus in the Original, but it is wrong caſt up; it ought to be – – 312,000

Q

The before-mentiond Armies, have the following
Forces to fight with, viz.

The combined Army, at Oſtend and
on the Sarre, Imperialiſts, Engliſh,
Dutch, Hanoverians, Pruſſians,
Heſſians, and Troops of the Ger-   *Men*
manic Circles   -   -   -   155,000
Combined Army on the Rhine, Pruſ-
ſians, Imperialiſts, Saxons, and the
Troops of the Circles   -   -   106,000
Army of hither Auſtria   -   -   16,000
Army of Piedmonteſe and Auſtrians   70,000
Spaniſh Biſcayan Army   -   ⸗   28,000
Ditto Catalonian   -   -   -   35,000
Royaliſt Army in Patua (unknown)

                               401,000 *

* Thus in the Original, but ought to be   410,000